Pawsome Foundations

A Beginner's Guide to Raising a Happy and Well-Trained Dog

Ella Quinn

Table of contents

Introduction

Educating your dog is a fundamental step to take. However, it is essential that this happens together and without too many demands or expectations. Each animal has its times, and it is not useful to continue to scold or beat it. In order to make him understand what we want from him, it is essential, first of all, to get to know your friend.

Yes, because as soon as you cross the threshold of the house, everything seems beautiful, easy to manage, and above all, simple. His needs are one of the priorities to be taught. And, it must be said, it is also one of the most difficult to understand. For various reasons: let's discover them together.

First of all, we have always said that it takes patience and perseverance when training a dog. The sooner it begins, the better it is for your pet and our quiet life. However, we must not be frightened, alarmed, or nervous if the dog does not immediately understand our requests. What matters is constancy and daily commitment.

Having said that, before letting your buddy into our house, we need to set up a place reserved only for his needs. That way, when we see him ready to evacuate, we can take him directly to that area. This will happen, above all, at the beginning of cohabitation, when both the dog and the owner do not know each other thoroughly.

Precisely for this reason, it would be a good idea to take him outside at least once every two hours, to make him understand that he must do his needs correctly. However, it is good to consider: if we arrive too late (or when the dog has already done his business), we avoid getting angry or scolding him or making him smell his pee. The moment has already passed, and our poor animal wouldn't understand the lesson anyway.

The same thing also applies to when we want to take the same buddy outside (even after the puppy has done his business at home): even, in this case, it would no longer make much sense, and the dog would not associate with his parents in any way.

Let us remember, therefore, that the initial phase (that of knowledge) is fundamental. Mutual knowledge is the primary step: the rest will come only later. It is essential to know that training a dog is a process that takes a lot of time. Precisely for this reason, it is good not to give up and not even feel depressed or crushed.

Finally, remember that the prize is essential. When your friend behaves well and does his needs in the area set up for them, let's remember to reward him correctly: greedy snacks, small morsels, and lots of pampering will make him understand which path must take every day.

Do you consider learning How to Train Your Dog Without punishments and Physical Corrections?

Are you looking for a fun and effective way to train your dog? Then keep reading...

Loving a dog is an easy task, but many frustrations link to a lack of obedience or nonpolite behaviors.

Are you afraid that your buddy will not listen in the moments you need it to?

A dog that can harm themselves or others is the last thing you want to happen. It is even worse when something like that may happen in public spaces. Jumping, chewing, biting, leash pulling, and excessive barking can be very embarrassing sometimes. As a result, many dogs end up staying at home without knowing how the world outside looks like.

Training your dog may be frustrating, but I can assure you that there is the end of the tunnel and that the feeling will not last forever. Just keep in mind that there are different ways of training a dog, and some are not good.

Applying the wrong methods will make you feel less like a pet parent and more like a dictator. They will not even help your dog develop good habits, and they will not help you develop that "best friend" bond with your dog...

Here is why I have condensed my 15 years of dog training experience in this book. With the simple strategies in this book, your dog will learn by having fun, just like kids.
Your dog will learn acceptable behavior faster, with fewer setbacks! And it will be a much more happy and pleasant experience for you both.

Inside this powerful section, you will discover:

- Why specific methods and tools are not only detrimental to training but also potentially harmful to your dog (and those around your dog).
- The 2 Basic Commands That Could Save Your Puppy's Life
- Chewing & Nipping: How To Curb Your Puppy From These 2 Annoying Behaviors
- The Right Kind Of Communication Necessary For Dog Training Success
- Quick Tips To Prevent Barking, Biting & Chewing
- How to Communicate better with your buddy by using specific body language tips
- Excessive Barking: how to quickly fix it
- ...And much more!

Dog training is not "magic." It is in science.

And that means that once you realize how a dog actually "works," you will be better able to communicate what you want in a way that your dog understands. If you are looking to have a brighter life-journey with your furry best friend, then turn the page and start reading..

Chapter One: Training Dogs For Beginners

To begin on the correct foot (and paw!) with your little guy, he will have to recognize what you anticipate from him. This will make him feel safe to meet the objectives spread out for him going ahead.

The establishment of preparation should be based on promoting feedback. Uplifting responses is the way toward giving a puppy (or individual!) compensation to energize the conduct you need, such as getting a check for getting down to business. The thought isn't to fix the conduct yet to prepare it utilizing something your pooch esteems. Abstain from utilizing discipline, for example, rope revisions or shouting. Discipline can make a canine confounded and uncertain about what is being asked of him. Remember that we can't anticipate that mutts should comprehend what they do not have the foggiest idea "only like you wouldn't expect a 2-year-old kid to realize how to tie his shoes. Persistence will go far in helping your new little dog figure out how to carry on.

Support can be anything your puppy likes. A great many people utilize little bits of a "high worth" nourishment for preparing treats" something extraordinary," for example, dried liver or even only their kibble. Shower acclaim or the opportunity to play with a most loved toy can likewise be utilized as a prize. Mutts must be instructed to like acclaim. If you give the canine a treat while saying "Great pooch!" in a cheerful voice, he will discover that acclaim is something to be thankful for and can be a prize. A few mutts likewise appreciate petting. Nourishment is regularly the most helpful approach to fortify conduct.

Doggies can start fundamental preparation beginning when they return home, for the most part around about two months old. Continually make instructional meetings brief" only 5 to 10 minutes" and consistently finish strong. On the remote possibility that your young doggie is experiencing difficulty learning another conduct, end the session by investigating something he knows and give him a lot of recognition and a significant award for his prosperity. On the off chance that your doggie gets exhausted or baffled, it will eventually be counterproductive to learning.

Instruct canine to come

You will need to start preparing a review (come when called) in a tranquil region and inside. Sit with your young doggie and state his name or "come." Each time you state "come/name," give your little dog a treat. He does not need to do anything yet. Just rehash the word and give a treat. Easy peasy!

Next, drop a treat on the floor close to you. When your little dog completes the treat on the ground, say his name once more. At the point when he looks into it, give him another treat. Rehash this two or multiple times until you can start hurling the treat somewhat further away, and he can pivot to confront you when you state his name. Abstain from rehashing your pup's name; saying it time after time when he does not react makes it simpler for him to overlook it. Instead, draw nearer to your little dog and return to a stage where he can be fruitful at reacting to his name the first run through.

When your little dog can pivot to confront you, start including development and making the game increasingly fun! Hurl a treat on the ground and remove a couple of fast advances while calling your pup's name. They should pursue you since pursue entertaining! When they get you, give them a ton of recognition, treats, or play with a pull toy. Coming to you ought to be enjoyable! Keep expanding on these games with longer separations and in different areas. When preparing outside (consistently in a sheltered, encased territory), it might be useful to keep your young doggie on a long rope from the start.

At the point when your little dog comes to you, do not connect and get him. This can be mistaking or terrifying for certain canines. If your doggie is hesitant, bow and face them sideways and offer him treats as you go after the neckline. Never call your puppy to rebuff! This will just instruct him that you are eccentric, and it is a smart thought to stay away from you. Continuously reward your canine intensely for reacting to their name, regardless of whether they have been up to insidiousness!

Show a puppy to heel.

Doggie preparing can be somewhat looser, with the objective being that they walk cordially on a free chain without pulling. A few mentors want to state "how about we go" or "forward" rather than "heel" when they train this simple method for strolling together.

Whatever signal you pick, be reliable, and consistently utilize a similar word. Regardless of whether your pup strolls on your left side or your right side is totally up to you. In any case, be predictable about where you need them, so they do not get confounded and figure out how to crisscross before you.

In the first place, ensure your young doggie is happy with wearing a chain. This can feel unusual from the outset, and a few pups may nibble the rope. Give your doggie treats as you put the chain on each time. At that point, remain beside your young doggie with the rope in a free circle and give him a few treats in succession for standing or sitting by your leg. Step advance and urge him to follow by giving another treat as he makes up for a lost time.

Keep offering treats to your pup at the degree of your knee or hip as you stroll forward. When he runs before you, essentially turn the other way, call him to you, and prize him set up. At that point, proceed. Slowly start giving treats further separated (from each progression to each other advance, each third step, etc.).

In the end, your pup will walk joyfully next to you at whatever point he is on his rope. Permit your puppy a lot of time to sniff and "enjoy the scenery" on your strolls. At the point when they have had their sniffing time, give the sign "How about we go!" in a cheerful voice and prize them for returning into position and strolling with you.

There are two unique strategies for indicating to your little dog what "sit" signifies.

The primary technique is called catching. Remain before your young doggie holding a portion of his pooch nourishment or treats. Be patient with him until he sits, tell him, "yes," then give him a snack. Then step in reverse or sideways to ask him to stand and hang tight for him to sit. Give them another treat when they sit. After a couple of reiterations, you can start saying "sit" directly as he starts to sit.

The following alternative is called attracting. Get down before your little dog, holding a treat as a draw. Put the treat directly before the puppy's nose; at that point, gradually lift the nourishment over his head. He will presumably sit down as he lifts his head to the treat. Let him eat the treat when his body touches the floor. Rehash a couple of times with the nourishment bait; at that point, expel the nourishment and utilize only your vacant hand, yet keep on compensating the young doggie after he sits. When he comprehends the hand sign to sit, you can start saying "sit" directly before giving the hand signal.

Never physically put your little dog into the sitting position; this can be befuddling or upsetting to certain mutts.
The most effective method to Teach a Dog to Stay
A pup who knows to "remain" prompt will stay sitting until you request that he get up by giving another sign, called the "discharge word." Staying set up is term conduct. The objective is to encourage your canine to stay sitting until the discharge prompt is given. At that point, start including separation.

In the first place, train the discharge word. Pick which word you will utilize, for example, "alright" or "free." Stand with your young doggie in a sit or a stand, hurl a treat on the floor, and state your assertion as he ventures forward to get the treat. Rehash this a few times until you can say the word first and afterward hurl the treat AFTER he starts to move. This shows the puppy that the discharge sign intends to move your feet.

At the point when your canine realizes the discharge sign and how to sit on prompt, turn and face him, put him in a sit, and give him a treat. Delay, and give him another treat for remaining in a sit, at that point discharge him. Step by step, increment the time you hold up between treats (it can sing the ABC's in your mind and stir your way up the letters in order). On the off chance that your canine gets up before the discharge sign, that is alright! It just means he is not prepared to sit for that long, so you can make it simpler by returning to a shorter time.

When your puppy can remain in a sit for a few seconds, you can start including separation. Spot him in a seat and state "remain," make one stride back, at that point step back to the little guy, give a treat, and your discharge word. Keep working in steps, keeping it simple enough that your canine can remain effective. Practice both confronting him and leaving with your back turned (which is increasingly sensible).

When your puppy can remain, you can steadily expand the separation. This is likewise valid for the "sit." The more positively he learns it, the more he can stay sitting. The key is not to anticipate perfection too early. Preparing objectives are accomplished in increases, so you may need to back off and center around each thing in turn. To ensure the preparation "sticks," sessions ought to be short and effective.

The most effective method to Teach a Dog to Lay Down (maybe put these sub-titles in bold or italics?)
"Down" can be instructed comparatively to "sit." You can trust that your canine will rest (start in an exhausting, little room, for example, a washroom can help) and catch the conduct by

strengthening your pup with a treat when he rests, give him his discharge sign to get back up (and consolation with a draw if necessary) and afterward sit tight for him to rest once more. When he is rapidly resting after standing up, you can start saying "down" directly before he does so.

You can likewise draw a down from a sit or remain by grasping a treat to the canine's nose and gradually carrying it to the floor. Give the treat when the pup's elbows contact the floor to begin. After a couple of practices, start carrying your vacant hand to the floor and giving the treat AFTER he rests. At the point when he can dependably follow your hand signal, start saying "down" as you move your hand.

Continue instructional courses short and fun. Finish strong if your puppy makes some troublesome memories learning or is "difficult," assess your preparation speed and the estimation of your prizes. Do you have to back off and make the means simpler, or does your pup need a more significant check for a more challenging exercise?

The "Fundamental 5" directions will give your young doggie a solid establishment for any future preparation.

What is more, if you and your young doggie keep on buckling down" and have a fabulous time" at preparing, some time or another, you may become compliance champs!

Canine Training for Beginners

Preparing upgrades your association with your canine and advances the bond you set up with him consistently. When you figure out how to speak with one another, you will show signs of improvement. Here are nine essential canine preparing ventures for fledglings:

1.   Enroll in Obedience Classes

Preparing takes practice, and the additional time and exertion you put into the procedure, the more you will receive in return. You might need to consider enlisting a private coach or consider pursuing an instructional course. Doggies typically begin in pup kindergarten. After that, you can join an acquiescence class for more seasoned doggies. Class size for little dogs ought to be constrained to eight to ten pooch and-handler groups per teacher. This proportion empowers the teacher to give each group enough consideration and time to react to questions or extraordinary preparing conditions.

During class, your little dog will become familiar with certain fundamentals, for example, sit, come, down, remain, and how to walk pleasantly on a chain. These basic exercises with an educator and different class members will show you the essentials while profiting from others' hardships.

2.   Use Positivity

Your puppy will react to your heading on the off chance that you make it fun. Creature behaviorists accept that the old methods for unforgiving rectifications may work on more than one occasion, yet they are regularly heartless and incapable over the long haul. Your pup will not comprehend why you are furious with him.

A year-long investigation by the University of Pennsylvania, distributed in the diary Applied Animal Behavior Science (Elsevier), indicated that forceful mutts who were prepared with forceful, fierce, or aversive preparing methods, for example, being gazed at, snarled at, moved onto their backs, or hit, proceeded with their forceful ways. Non-aversive preparing techniques, for example, exercise or rewards, were instrumental in diminishing or taking out violent reactions. Encouraging feedback tells your canine that you are satisfied with him, and he will rehash that conduct whenever. Prizes can comprise nourishment, toys, or petting, relying upon what your pup reacts to best. When he gets it, reward him with nourishment, toys, or petting just a portion of the time (however verbally acclaim him unfailingly). Along these lines, he will strive to satisfy you, trusting that he will get a prize.

3. Keep Training Sessions Short

Start showing your pooch great habits a couple of days after he has gotten an opportunity to subside into the family unit. Keep your preparation exercises short" for around 10 to 15 minutes at every session. You can rehash the session later on around the same time. However, everyone ought to be brief. Plan to participate in a few instructional courses a day because of no little dog figures out how to accomplish something flawlessly in just one take.

4. Use Small Treats

It's a smart thought to give him some little treats as remunerations for preparing. You can utilize delicate business nourishment treats estimated for little dogs, bits of string cheddar, or little bits of cut-up wiener that he can swallow immediately. Please keep away from hard, crunchy treats since they require a significant period to bite. Offer treats to your young doggie quickly" inside a large portion of a moment of him finishing the exemplary conduct. The quicker you affirm the conduct you need, the simpler it is for your young doggie to comprehend what you are attempting to educate him. When you give the prize, tail it up by saying, "Great kid!"

Keep away from the snare of distributing treats during an instructional meeting because your doggie looks charming. He will work more enthusiastically to satisfy you on the off chance that he realizes that he is getting a prize than if he has not earned it. On the remote possibility that he does not accomplish something you like, do not holler or rebuff. Essentially retain the prize.

5. Say a Cue Word Only Once

State a prompt word, as "sit" or "down," just once. Mutts are savvy, so they hear your direction and can tail it the first run through. Rehashing the prompt word on different occasions does not enable your puppy to hone his listening abilities, and like a young person, he will block you out.

6. Schedule Training Before Meals

Calendar your instructional meeting before your pup's traditional dinner. Along these lines, he may give nearer consideration to the guidelines with the goal that he can gain a delicious chomp.

#7: Choose a Training Time With No Distractions

Pick a period for preparing when nobody will intrude on you, and you do not feel rushed. Turn your mobile phone off and disregard, noting the doorbell on the off chance that it rings. This will give you quality time to commit to the preparation procedure.

For the initial sessions, pick a room in the house that is sufficiently enormous to move around. At the point when your canine makes sense of what you need him to do, take your preparation exercises outside, ideally to a fenced-in zone, or keep him on a chain when you are in an unfenced zone. Interruptions will compete for your young doggie's consideration, so you will have to turn out to be more fascinating than the road clamor, a quick-moving squirrel, or the aroma of recently cut grass.

7. Do not Train When Puppy's Not in the Mood

Try not to prepare your young doggie when he is hot, tired, or in lively recess. You need him engaged and enthusiastic for an instructional meeting.

8.   Do not Get Angry With Your Puppy

On the off possibility that you will become disappointed with preparing your young doggie, do not blow up with him. Just discreetly end the session and attempt again later in the day. Numerous canines become apprehensive and will quit focusing on their mentors if they are shouted at. They can get terrified of preparing and conclude that the following headings are not for them. Remain without a care in the world so your doggie will learn in a positive domain.

Instructions to Train Your Dog

Need assistance with hound preparing? Consider finding support from a canine coach. Attempt group classes as well as private exercises, and check here for tips on right pooch preparation.

House Training and Crate Training

Except if you intend to keep your pup outside - you will have to show your canine where to take out. In this way, house preparing (likewise called housebreaking or potty preparing) is one of the main things you have to take a look at with your canine. Case preparation can be an exceptionally supportive piece of the preparation procedure. This incorporates house preparing just as numerous different regions of preparing:

Container Training Dogs and Puppies: Here are the fundamentals of preparing your pooch or pup to acknowledge and even appreciate the case. Not exclusively will it help with housebreaking, yet it will likewise give your pup his very own position.

This is the most efficient way to train your dog at home: When it comes down to it, house preparing isn't that confounded. However, this does not mean it's simple. Consistency and tirelessness are essential during the housebreaking procedure.

Compliant/Excitement Urination in Dogs: If your canine is as yet having mishaps in the house, it might be more than a fundamental housebreaking issue. Your puppy may pee out of hunger or to express compliant conduct.

Chain Training Dogs and Puppies

Other than how most regions have chain laws, there will be times when keeping your canine on a rope is for his own sake. Try to understand how to acquaint your canine or little dog with the chain. Then show him how to walk appropriately on the rope, even close to you on a bicycle. A free rope walk shows your puppy not to pull or jump on the rope, making the experience increasingly pleasant for both you and your canine.

Step by step instructions to socialize with canines

Socialization implies preparing your young doggie or grown-up pooch to acknowledge new individuals, creatures, and different places by presenting him to these things. Mingled hounds are more averse to create conduct issues and are commonly more invited by others. Socialization can either way help forestall the improvement of fears.

Most importantly, mingling your canine or young doggie will make him a more joyful, all the more polite pooch.

Clicker Training for Dogs

Clicker preparing, a typical type of encouraging feedback, is a straightforward and powerful canine preparing technique. It is still acceptable to prepare your canine without clicker preparation; numerous individuals think it is accommodating. With clicker preparation, you can, without much of a stretch and viably show your pup a wide range of essential and proper directions and stunts. It is quick and straightforward to understand how to clicker train your canine.

Fundamental Commands and Fun Tricks

Some fundamental canine preparing directions and pooch devices that each canine should know as: come here, bark, drop it, remain, back up, and so on. Essential directions give your pooch structure. Also, they can assist you with defeating fundamental pooch conduct issues and will help guard your canine.

What's a better time than flaunting your canine's cool stunts?! Pooch stunts are an extraordinary method to take your canine preparation to the following level and give your pup some psychological incitement.

Sealing Behaviors and Troubleshooting

Sealing is the last advance in preparing your canine to do any new conduct. Figure out how to verify practices, so your pup will be as respectful at the recreation center or a companion's home as he is in your very own lounge.

Remember, since you have arrived at the last phases of preparing, it does not imply that conduct issues won't manifest. Find out about the most widely recognized pooch conduct issues and how to handle them. These points will assist you in exploring this piece of the preparation procedure:

Sealing Behaviors: Practice practices in an assortment of circumstances with various degrees of interruption. Without sealing, your puppy may act well in your parlor yet appear to overlook all his preparation when he is outside the house.

Show Your Dog Self-Control: This technique shows your pup that nothing in life is free; however, he needs to gain things like nourishment and consideration through compliance.

Average Dog Behavior Problems: Understanding potential conduct issues can help you recognize and address them before things gain out of power.

Canine Behavior Management Versus Dog Training: While hound conduct the board and pooch preparing are two unique things, they are not fundamentally unrelated. Conduct the executives is a significant piece of any pooch preparing program.

Propelled Dog Training

When your canine has aced every one of the essentials, you can think about proceeding onward to develop stunts further. These exercises will help keep your puppy dynamic, fit, and intellectually animated. Besides, they will help fortify the bond you share with your canine buddy.

Recall that preparation is a continuous procedure. You will never be wrapped up. It is critical to continue dealing with compliance, preparing for the duration of the life of your puppy. Individuals who become familiar with a language at a young age yet quit communicating in that language may overlook a lot of it as they become more seasoned. The equivalent goes for your canine: use it or lose it. Going through even the most essential devices and directions will help them remain crisp in your canine's psyche. Besides, it is an extraordinary method to invest energy with your canine.

Instructions to Train Your Dog

Appropriate preparation and socialization are among your canine's essential needs. It is imperative to begin preparing your canine as quickly as time permits.

Need assistance with hound preparing? Consider finding support from a canine coach. Attempt bunch classes and additionally private exercises, and check here for tips on proper canine preparation.

House Training and Crate Training

You will have to show your puppy where to dispose of it. This way, house preparing (additionally called housebreaking or potty preparing) is one of the main things you have to deal with your canine. Box preparation can be a useful piece of the preparation procedure. This incorporates house preparing just as numerous different zones of preparing:

Container Training Dogs and Puppies: Here are the essentials of preparing your pooch or pup to acknowledge and even appreciate the carton. Not exclusively will it help with housebreaking, yet it will likewise give your canine his very own position.

Step by step instructions to train your dog a: When it comes down to it, house preparing is not that chaotic, yet this doesn't mean it's simple. Consistency and persistence are essential during the housebreaking procedure.

Accommodating/Excitement Urination in Dogs: If your puppy is as yet having mishaps in the house, it might be more than a straightforward housebreaking issue. Your puppy may pee out of enthusiasm or to express compliant conduct.

Chain Training Dogs and Puppies

Other than how most territories have chain laws, there will be times when keeping your canine on a rope is for his very own well-being. Figure out how to acquaint your puppy or pup with a rope. Then show him how to walk appropriately on the chain, even next to you on a bicycle. A free chain walk shows your canine not to pull or jump on ‹the rope, making the experience progressively charming for both you and your pup.

Dark lab doggie on a chain, watching his proprietor.

Socialization implies preparing your doggie or grown-up pooch to acknowledge new individuals, creatures, and different places by presenting him to these things. Mingled hounds are less inclined to create conduct issues and are commonly more invited by others. Socialization can likewise help forestall the advancement of fears and fears.

Mingling your pooch or doggie will make him a more joyful, all the more polite canine.

Clicker Training for Dogs

Clicker preparing, a typical type of encouraging feedback, is a raw and compelling pooch preparing strategy. Even though it is still acceptable to prepare your canine without clicker preparing, numerous individuals think it's supportive. With clicker preparation, you can, without much of a stretch and viably show your canine a wide range of fundamental directions and stunts. It is quick and straightforward to understand how to clicker train your canine.

Fundamental Commands and Fun Tricks

Some fundamental canine preparing directions and pooch deceives that each pooch should know as: come here, talk, drop it, remain, back up, and so forth. Fundamental directions give your pooch structure. Furthermore, they can assist you with beating everyday canine conduct issues and will help protect your puppy. (Repeated section?)

Step by step instructions to Train Your Dog to Stay

What is a better time than flaunting your canine's cool stunts?! Pooch stunts are an extraordinary method to take your canine preparation to the following level and give your pup some psychological incitement.

Sealing Behaviors and Troubleshooting

Sealing is the last advance in preparing your canine to do any new conduct. Figure out how to verification practices, so your pup will be as loyal at the recreation center or a companion's home as he is in your lounge.

Since you arrived at the last steps of preparing, it does not imply that conduct issues won't manifest. Find out about the most widely recognized pooch conduct issues and how to handle them. These hints will assist you in exploring this piece of the preparation procedure:

Sealing Behaviors: Practice practices in an assortment of circumstances with various degrees of interruption. Your canine may carry on well in your lounge; however, it appears to overlook all his preparation when he is outside the house.

Show Your Dog Self-Control: This technique shows your pup that nothing in life is free; however, he needs to get things like nourishment and consideration through dutifulness.

Regular Dog Behavior Problems: Understanding potential conduct issues can help you identify and address them before things gain out of power.

Canine Behavior Management Versus Dog Training: While hound conduct the executives and pooch preparation are two unique things, they are not unrelated. Conduct the executives is a significant piece of any pooch preparing program.

Propelled Dog Training

When your canine has aced every one of the nuts and bolts, you can think about proceeding onward to further developed stunts. These exercises will help keep your puppy dynamic, fit, and intellectually invigorated. Furthermore, they will help fortify the bond you share with your canine friend.

Recall that preparation is a continuous procedure. You will never be wrapped up. It is critical to continue dealing with submission, preparing for the duration of the life of your canine. Individuals who get familiar with a language at a young age yet quit communicating in that language may overlook a lot of it as they become more established. The equivalent goes for your pooch: use it or lose it. Going through even the most essential deceives and directions will help them remain crisp in your canine's psyche. Besides, it's an extraordinary method to invest energy with your pup. (repeat section)

7 Most Popular Dog Training Methods

There are such vast numbers of well-known canine preparing techniques out there that it tends to be baffling to discover which will be which and what strategy will be best for both your puppy and you as a proprietor.

You are not the only one on the off chance that you think it's staggering and confounding. There is even a lot of difference inside the expert pooch preparing network about which strategies are successful and moral. A few techniques cover or are utilized couple for the best outcomes.

1.Encouraging feedback

Uplifting feedback is a strategy advanced via mentors like Dawn Sylvia-Stasiewicz, who prepared the Obamas' puppy, Bo. The hypothesis behind it is genuinely direct. Mutts will rehash excellent conduct when it's prize trails it. Awful conduct does not get a prize or affirmation. If an amendment needs to occur, it comes as the evacuation of remunerations, similar to a toy or treats being removed. Harsh censures or physical disciplines are not fundamental. This preparation technique starts with compensating ideal conduct promptly, inside seconds after it occurs. That way, the canine comes to connect the conduct with the prize.

A few mentors join this strategy with clicker preparation (see number three beneath). This offers the pooch an unmistakable hint of the precise minute the conduct was finished. Directions likewise should be short and to the point. Sit. Remain. Come.

Uplifting feedback requires consistency. In this manner, everybody in your family unit needs to utilize similar directions and prize framework. Start with ceaseless rewards each time your puppy makes the best decision. At that point, slowly move to discontinuous prizes as the conduct gets reliable. At times apprentice coaches inadvertently reward terrible conduct. For instance, they may let the canine outside when they start yelping at a squirrel or another puppy. Just needed practices get rewards, which can incorporate treats, toys, acclaim, and pets? It can likewise be difficult to overload when your puppy is adapting, so utilize little treats when you are remunerating with nourishment. This technique is extraordinary for learning directions; however, you need tolerance for adjusting undesirable practices.

2. Logical Training

Science-based canine preparation can be hard to characterize as it depends on data that is ceaselessly assembling and evolving. It expects to comprehend mutts' tendency, their capacity to be adapted, and remunerations and disciplines' viability.

Creature behaviorists are continually making new investigations and tests to shape our comprehension of canine brain science. Mentors depend on these investigations to work with hounds. Before conduct is adjusted, everything about that conduct must be comprehended.

Since science-based canine preparation is so expansive, it's difficult to pinpoint a general procedure behind it. Different preparing types utilize many strategies utilized in logical pooch preparation. Generally, there is a dependence on operant molding, which, for the most part, incorporates uplifting feedback and, less regularly, a few types of discipline.

Some logical mentors accept that it is also essential to figure out how to reinforce excellent conduct without remunerations and depend on hound brain research to discover approaches to improve off-rope connections among proprietors and their puppies. Logical preparation depends on making a decent arrangement of research and staying refreshed on the most recent examinations. Therefore, it might be best for proficient coaches, and different types of preparing as of now utilize a considerable lot of those techniques.

Additionally, growing new strategies dependent on research may not be fitting for everybody. It's a smart thought for hound proprietors to remain educated and focus on new research when it gets accessible.

3. Clicker Training

Clicker preparing is likewise founded on operant molding and depends vigorously on indistinguishable standards from uplifting feedback. Clicker preparing might be gathered in as a technique for encouraging feedback instead of as its type of preparing.

It depends on utilizing a gadget to make a snappy, sharp commotion, for example, a whistle or, as the name recommends, a clicker to move toward a canine when needed conduct is practiced.

The benefit of utilizing clicker preparing is that it flags the careful minute the exemplary conduct is done and precisely what is being reimbursed. Mentors would then be able to utilize the clicker to shape new practices and include verbal directions. Initially, the canine should be adapted to realize that a tick implies a prize is coming. At that point, the puppy can connect conduct with a tick and a prize. At long last, the verbal order can be acquainted with the structure of another affiliation.

This is an excellent strategy for adapting new deceives, and it can help shape the nuts and bolts into increasingly convoluted errands. Numerous expert coaches utilize this technique.

While it is incredible for adopting new practices, clicker preparing is not appropriate for checking undesirable practices. When utilized close by other preparing strategies, it tends to ensure you have a well-prepared, polite pooch.

4. Electronic Training

A youthful Boston terrier hound is watching eagerly, just wondering. Electronic preparation depends on utilizing an electric neckline that conveys a stun or a shower of citronella when a puppy isn't playing out an ideal assignment. It's generally utilized for preparing the right way off when a chain can't be utilized.

For instance, stun collars can prepare a canine to remain inside the limits of an un-fenced yard. Remote collars can instruct puppies to work in fields or do chasing work. Individuals who utilize these gadgets guarantee that there is less danger of a puppy getting injured than stifle collars or other mechanical gadgets. There are numerous issues with this preparation technique. It depends on discipline for awful conduct rather than remunerations, which means a canine realizes what they should not do instead of what they ought to do.

Another issue is that it can put a lot of pressure and lead to changeless uneasiness issues for hounds. The gadgets are regularly utilized by unpracticed proprietors and accordingly are abused. This can cause a great deal of superfluous torment, both physically and mentally, for hounds. Proficient canine mentors may see wanted outcomes from electronic preparing; however, it's certainly not for use by familiar proprietors. Numerous options put mutts under far less pressure and torment. In case you are going to utilize an electronic gadget, counsel an expert about appropriate utilization and think about an elective type of conduct redress.

5. Model-Rival or Mirror Training

The model-rival technique for preparing depends on the way that canines learn by perception. Giving a model of right conduct or an opponent to seek assets, hounds figure out how to mirror practices.

A mentor may have another human go about as the model, applauding them to finish undertakings on the direction or scolding them for undesirable conduct. The canine, as a spectator, gains what to do effectively from the model.

The model can likewise go about as an opponent, contending to do the correct errand for an ideal toy or treat as a prize, urging the canine to get on the undertaking and achieve it all the more rapidly. Mirror preparing depends on a similar rule, utilizing the pooch proprietor as a model, at that point offering awards for imitating excellent conduct. It utilizes the pooch's ordinary senses to work socially as opposed to neutralizing them. The puppy learns by model. This preparation strategy works with a comparable degree of achievement as encouraging feedback and operant molding. Be that as it may, a few coaches may think that it's increasingly common and ideal.

Suppose your canine has a solid bond with you and can invest a great deal of energy watching you and chasing after you. In that case, this might be a strategy that you discover more agreeable than adhering to ordinary instructional courses.

6. Alpha Dog Or Dominance

Back perspective on a man strolling a gathering of mutts

Alpha pooch or predominance preparing depends on a canine's instinctual pack mindset to make a relationship of accommodation and strength.

The hypothesis recommends that mutts consider them to be their packs and follow a social pecking order, as seen in hostage wolf packs. When a puppy considers themselves the alpha, they have to figure out how rather regard their human as the alpha and submit.

A few strategies utilized in this procedure incorporate understanding pooch non-verbal communication and reacting like manner, anticipating certainty and authority, and going first regarding eating, going into or leaving rooms, or strolling on the rope.

If your puppy needs to go out, at that point, they need to sit before you open the entryway. On the remote possibility that they need to eat, at that point, they need to stand by smoothly while you get ready nourishment. For the most part, with alpha preparing, you do not permit your puppy on furniture with you, including the bed. You likewise do not get down to your canine's eye level. That is because these are signs that your puppy has equivalent remaining in the relationship. You are in control; you are predominant.

Cesar Millan promoted this preparation strategy. In any case, he here and there consolidates strength preparing with different strategies when proper. Some advanced coaches state this procedure is obsolete, as new research has indicated that mutts do not depend on pack mindset as recently suspected. The wolves' pack dynamic is not organized in the wild a similar way; it was the point at which the creatures were seen in captivity.

Chapter Two: Learning The First Commands, Treats And Sitting

Be consistent when training your puppy, or he will get confused as to when or if to listen.

If you tell him to sit, make him sit.

If you tell him to stay, make him stay.

If you do not want him on the couch, never let him on the couch.

If you do not want him jumping on you, do not let him jump up.

You have to do it when it needs to be done, or you will pay the price tenfold! <u>Basic commands are the foundation of obedience training</u>. You could sign your puppy up for professional obedience training lessons, but you may want to attempt teaching the commands on your own first. If your puppy catches on quickly, you could save some money by teaching the necessary skills on your own. Following are effective strategies for teaching all of the basic commands. **Remember to use the same word** every time you work on command. Your dog will learn what you want them to do according to that exact sound, so the terms cannot be switched up. Stay consistent!

→ **"Come"**

This is typically the first command you will teach your puppy. You can teach it simultaneously with **"sit"** and **"stay."** You are essentially telling your puppy to come to you. The key is to teach your puppy that coming to you is a pleasant experience. You never call your puppy to you and then put them on a leash, throw them right into the crate, or otherwise send a signal of punishment. Instead, call them to you and give them a small treat for a prompt response. Love on them. Slip them a small treat. Start by giving treats just for coming when called, and then start giving them only when they come and sit as commanded. Finally, wean out the treats, so they get used to coming just for a pat on the head and a bit of attention. Work with this command throughout your puppy's life. By adulthood, they should be well trained to come to you on command.

→ **"Sit"**

You can use small treats and praise and love to get your puppy to come to you and sit on command. Your goal should be to train them to sit and stay, so work with these two commands together. Start by gently pushing down on the backside of the puppy while giving this command. It would be best if you only had to do this a couple of times before catching on to what **"sit"** means.

After that:

1. Command them to sit after getting their attention and give them a small treat.

2. Start by rewarding just the seat. You can then start rewarding only when they sit and stay for a couple of seconds.

3. Start this training at home without any distractions.

With time you can practice around other people, in public places, and with other distractions that will make the puppy want to get up and run. Eventually, you want your puppy to come to you, sit down, and stay put. A well-trained puppy will eventually grow into a well-trained adult dog able to stay by its owner's side even when there are serious distractions, such as a bird playing in a puddle nearby. That level of training takes time, so be patient.

→ "Shake"

This is probably the easiest trick to teach your puppy. Make your buddy sit in front of you. Tell him "shake" and grab his front paw and give it a gentle shake. Then give him a treat. Do this a couple of times. After the fifth or sixth time, tell him "shake" and just put your hand in front of him and see if he will offer his paw. If he does, really praise him and give him a treat. If not, grab his paw and keep repeating until he will offer his paw on his own.

→ Potty training

It is time to potty train your puppy by use Clicker training. This method is based on the famous "clicker training." Instead of using the clicker for every aspect of training, you will use it only for potty training, thereby increasing its effectiveness. If you do not have a clicker, visit your nearest pet store. You can use this method whether you have a puppy or dog, work all day, or are at home, or if you've already started a different potty training method and it hasn't worked. Throw out the other ideas you have had about potty training and start fresh. This method is so easy to teach, and most puppies and dogs will catch on too quickly.

Remember, though, that your puppy will need to have a good diet and a strict schedule. No puppy will become potty trained if fed "less than quality" food and fed whenever. You need to be completely dedicated, no matter how tired you are! Remember, a puppy learns only what he has been taught. Your puppy's good behavior, or lack of, reflects directly on you!

Before you begin with this method, you need to set your puppy up for success. Since your puppy is young, chances are he can't hold it for more than a few hours at a time. We would be very cruel of if we expect him to hold it all day, so be prepared to clean up messes until he is around 3-5 months of age. To help control where he messes in the house, you will need to set up a room or a large crate. These will be large enough for him to have areas to play, sleep, and mess. If we do not give him room to do these things, he will probably develop the nasty habit of messing with where he sleeps. This is a tough habit to break, so let us prevent it from the very beginning. If you use a room or exercise pen, it will work well if you use a crate for him to sleep in. This will prepare him for when he is older, and you want to crate him when you leave. When you set up the area that he will use when alone, be sure he has something comfortable to sleep on and the material you want him to mess outside normally. Suppose you want him always to place a piece of sod in his area. One-piece should last nearly a week if you clean up the poop. You want to leave the urine smell in the sod since this will attract your puppy back to the sod. If you prefer, he always goes on the cement outside, gets a thin slab of cement for his area. Again, clean off the poop, and every few days, rinse the slab with plain water.

Now we are ready to begin! If you have not brought your puppy home yet, plan on starting this from the second you pick him up. If you already have your puppy, start this when you have a few full days to work on it. First, we need to associate the clicker with something outstanding. This is one of the few times you will hear me say to use treats when training, but there is no better reward for a puppy than a tasty treat!

And what behavior other than going to the bathroom outside deserves something this good? Grab your puppy, the clicker, and a few treats you know your puppy likes. It will be advisable to do this outside on the surface you want him to use, at his designated potty spot, since you will always be clicking and treating his behavior outside.

Just click a few times, then give him a treat. Please choose how many times you will click the clicker, so he knows what he's doing well every time. Once or twice should suffice. Be sure only to give him a small piece of the treat. Please do not give him a whole mouthful. Continue to click and treat every few minutes. Once he hears the clicks and looks to you for a treat, you know, he is caught on. Now we wait until he goes to the bathroom. As soon as he starts to pee or poop, click the clicker. However, you have decided on it many times. When he is finished, please give him a treat and praise him. Put your clicker away until the next time you take him out to the bathroom. Repeat this every time he goes.

Now you are probably wondering how to handle it when he goes to the house. Well, you do nothing but clean it up.

Provided you click and treat every time he goes to the bathroom outside, he will catch that good thing happen when he goes outside, but nothing happens when he goes into the house. Before long, he will want to go outside all the time to go to the bathroom and get a treat. By using a few days to get him used to his spot outside on the surface you have chosen, chances are he will go on that same surface in the house. If he does not, try making his indoor mess area a little bigger or placing a small chunk of sod where he has previously gone pee on top of his indoor sod. Before long, you should have a puppy that willingly holds it until he can get outside.

NOTE: Do not expect too much from a puppy under 12-16 weeks old or a small breed puppy, though. Young and tiny puppies are not physically capable of holding it that long.

This should only be started after at least two weeks of no accidents in the house and your pup letting you know consistently that he needs to go out. We can now assume that your puppy understands that he is expected to go to the bathroom outside and that he will let you know it, so it should be safe to begin! Start this on a weekend morning or anytime you will have a few days to dedicate to this.

Take him out as you usually would in the morning. Click and treat as usual for this time. The next time you take him out, do not click but give a treat—couple this with plenty of praise. Take him back in and wait until the next time he needs to go out. Click and treat for this one. Do the click and treat for every other bathroom break for the rest of the day. If he seems okay with everything and is still going to the door to be let out, we can move on to the next day with no accidents in the house. If he backslides even once with either not letting you know he needs to go out or going to the bathroom in the house, go back to click and treat every time. He is not ready.

Give him a few days and try again. If everything went smoothly your first day, click and treat every third bathroom break.

Continue this for a few days, and if all is well, try eliminating the click and treat altogether for one day. If he has accidents in the house, go back a step. If all goes well, forget the click and treat for a few days and monitor his behavior. If he seems okay with the new arrangement, pat yourself on the back! You now have a potty trained puppy!

If your puppy makes a mistake in the house, go back one step, and continue working on that particular step for a few days. Some puppies may catch on to this right away, and others may take weeks or even months. Remember that you should not use the clicker for any other training. You do not want to confuse him, do you?

You can alter this method to fit your needs for other potty training. If you want to train your pup to mess in a litter box, click every time he goes in it. Follow the same guidelines, except for teaching him how to let you know he needs to go out. Or, if you have a doggy door, you can teach this method with much quicker results. Set your pup's pen up in front of the doggy door when you are gone, and he will be potty trained in no time! First, you must teach him to go out the doggy door. This is a matter of merely coaxing him through it while you hold it open to get his dinner. Do this a few times until he seems okay with it. Then close the door and have someone coax him through to the other side. This should not take much more than a few times. When teaching using a doggy door, keep in mind that you will still need to go out with him to click and treat. Let him go out the doggy door, and once he is through, you go out behind out.

Consult your vet if you feel your puppy is going way too much or not enough because some potty training problems are caused by the puppy or dog being sick. Do not expect too much from your puppy either. He is a puppy and will do what comes naturally or what was unintentionally taught to him. It's your job to teach him what is and isn't acceptable behavior. Do not slack off because you feel your puppy is stupid and incapable of learning or because you've just had it trying to teach him to go outside for three weeks, and he's still missing in the house.

All puppies can and will learn if given the proper instruction and time to learn. So, get ready to begin properly potty training your puppy! Before we begin, please take note of these potty training do's and don'ts.

Potty pieces of training do's
- Take your puppy out when he wakes up, after eating and drinking, when you first get home, and after play sessions. Take him outside through the same door.
- Take him to the same spot.
- Bring him back in through the same door.
- Take your puppy out on a leash.

- Clean up messes inside with a solution of half vinegar and half water.
- Choose a phrase as his "bathroom" signal and use it as soon as you get him to his spot.
- Leave a few stools in his bathroom area.
- Rush your puppy outside if he starts to mess in the house.
- Keep him on a set schedule for feeding, walking, etc.

Potty Training Don'ts
- Do not rub your puppy's nose in his mess.
- Please do not leave him in his crate for more extended periods than he can handle.
- Do not scold him for making a mess in the house. Do not hit your puppy for messing in the house. Please do not play with him before he goes to the bathroom. Do not let him have the run of the house before he's entirely trustworthy.
- Do not scold your puppy if he starts to mess in the house.
- Do not use newspaper when potty training. They are messy and confuse your pup.
- Do not use different doors to take him outside and back in.
- Do not ignore your puppy's need to go out, no matter how tired you are.

Chapter Three: Exercises For A Healthy Physical And Mental Condition For Your Dog And Breed Selection

Preparing Game 1: Wild Sits

The most effective method to play: Taught when a canine comprehends the idea of "sit," Wild Sits starts by having the pooch on-chain while the proprietor goes around cheering, bouncing all over, and getting the canine irritated up. (Note: If a puppy is docile, apprehensive, or touchy, mitigate the ferocity. The objective is an energized, not alarmed pooch.) Then, mid-cavort, the proprietor will teach the canine to sit. (This should be possible with a treat if the dog is a pup or new to preparing.) He most likely will not comply with the first run-through or two. However, after a little practice, he will have the option to go from acting hyper to sitting quietly in direction.

The advantages: Besides the cardio exercise you and your pup are getting during this activity, you are showing your canine to hear you out while he's in a condition of hyperactivity. How regularly has your puppy gone crazy when the doorbell rings or when he sees individuals in the city and disregarded your arguing for him to sit? Presently you are showing him how to pull himself once more into a responsive and submissive perspective. How extraordinary is that?

Preparing Game 2: Cardio Twist

Step by step instructions to play: Those who know about deftness realize this activity as weave shafts. However, any canine proprietor can show her pet to do it to have some good times, chip away at coordination, and get a cardio exercise. Nearly set up "shafts" utilizing collapsing seats, orange cones, unused latrine uncloggers, or even individuals, and educate your canine to heel close by you as you weave between them, changing your pace from quick to slow. Consider it being like a slalom course in skiing.

The advantages: Your canine needs to focus more diligently on tailing you as you rapidly alter course. Additionally, because he will remain at your left side as you rapidly weave left and right, he will need to change his pace to be increasingly slow, separately, which is the thing that your fitness coach would call interim preparing. Include considerably all the more an exercise by running the whole course.

Give exchanging a shot of one of your ordinary instructional courses with these games. Notwithstanding having a well-prepared and well-practiced pup, you will likewise receive the rewards of getting more cardio. And keeping in mind that I am not proposing this can be an option in contrast to heading off to the recreational center. I am talking as a matter of the fact that your association with your pup and your physicality will improve significantly.

Enhancing Your Dog's Life

Weariness and abundance of vitality are two standard explanations behind conduct issues in hounds. This bodes well since they are intended to have dynamic existences. Wild canines spend about 80% of their waking hours chasing and rummaging for nourishment. Residential canines have been aiding and working nearby us for a great many years, and most are reproduced for a particular reason, for example, chasing, cultivating, or security. For instance, retrievers and pointers were reared to find and bring game and waterfowls. Like coonhounds and beagles, fragile dogs were reproduced to discover bunnies, foxes, and other little prey. Canines like German shepherds, collies, steers, mutts, and sheepdogs were bred into domesticated group animals. Regardless of whether dogs worked for us or rummaging alone, their endurance once relied upon heaps of activity and critical thinking.

Today that is altogether changed. Presently the most well-known set of working responsibilities for hounds is Couch Potato! While we are away at work throughout the day, they rest. When we get back home, we serve them free nourishment in a bowl," no exertion required from them. They eat a more significant number of calories than they can utilize. The outcome is hounds who are exhausted senseless, frequently overweight and have an excess of vitality. It's an ideal formula for conduct issues.

What Does Your Dog Need?

It's not essential to leave your place of employment, take up duck chasing, or get yourself many sheep to keep your canine out of difficulty. Be that as it may, we urge you to discover approaches to practice her cerebrum and body. Peruse on for some fun, down to earth approaches to enhance your puppy's life, both when you are near and when you are most certainly not. You will see that these thoughts go far toward keeping your pooch glad and more straightforward to live with. Evaluate a couple and see what you and your canine appreciate most.

Tips for Alone Time

Since we as a whole have occupied existences, our pooches regularly wind up spending a decent part of their day home alone. Give your canine "occupations" to do when she is without anyone else's input. She will be more averse to think of her particular manners to involve her time, such as unstuffing your sofa, assaulting the garbage, or biting on your preferred pair of shoes. Furthermore, she will be more averse to energetically handle you when you get back home after she's gone through a day sitting idle, however energizing her batteries!

6 Great Ways to Challenge Your Dog's Mind

Much the same as individuals, hounds get exhausted with the regular old ordinary everyday practice. Keeping them slow-witted and continually presenting them to new things is similarly as significant as going for them for strolls and practicing them. Exhausted canines create harmful practices and take their negative vitality out on items like your furnishings.

Here are some inventive approaches to animate your pooch's psyche so they do not get exhausted and get rowdy:

1. Work on another stunt

Each time you draw in your canine in an instructional course, you are furnishing him with a psychological test. Quest around for new deceives to chip away at. In case you are prepared to move past the fundamental directions, look at books, check the Internet, and approach a mentor for thoughts for new deceives and preparing opinions.

"My canine, Vince just as of late turned 4-years of age, and I at last selected him in acquiescence school. It has changed both our lives. Presently on days where I work him on new devices, I have seen that his personality has quieted down. Testing him intellectually makes him significantly less restless when all is said in done. He has gotten progressively loose around different canines. Vince is evidence that old canines can adopt new devices." "Sara Hicks

2. Play with intelligent games or plays with your canine

Buy a doggie table game or a canine riddle to challenge your little guy. Draw in your pup in a round of Dog Memory or Dog Dominos. Give your puppy one of the many toys that enable you to shroud treats and items inside and draw in your canine to make sense of how to function them out. "This sounds senseless; however, I purchased this prepackaged game that I saw at the store for my pooch snickers and I to play together. I put treats underneath a peg, and she needs to make sense of which ones to lift to discover where the treats are. There is another adaptation where I conceal the treats with this bit of plastic, and Snickers needs to turn the board around to reveal the treats. It truly challenges her, and I see her cerebrum endeavoring to make sense of everything." "Donna Marr

3. Get things done with your canine

Indeed, even a fast race to the letterbox, a stopover at a companion's home, or a turn through the vehicle wash will put your puppy up close and personal with an assortment of energizers.

"Indeed, even simply taking Ryker for a vehicle ride or to the vehicle wash is animating for him. He gets the opportunity to see loads of various sights and sounds and experience new circumstances. He cherishes proceeding to get so energized. What is more, I can see his cerebrum functioning as it takes it all in. What is more, when we get back home, he falls right snoozing, even though it wasn't physically saddling." "Jennifer Brody.

4. Give your pup a vocation to do

Mutts are reared to finish assignments, for example, chasing and grouping. When they are not ready to satisfy these kinds of obligations, they can get eager. Draw in your puppy in a round of Frisbee. Get him associated with a game like nimbleness or Flyball. Take him for a long walk, climb, or swim. Secure positions that satisfy your canine's breed. For instance, if you have a retriever, nothing will leave it more fulfilled than a healthy round of getting.

"I can take my puppy for a walk or a run, yet what truly makes her the most joyful is a great round of getting. I take a tennis racket to the canine park and hit a ball the extent that I can. She will take it back to me again and again like it's her activity." "John Kurma.

5. Acquaint your puppy with new faces

Each time your puppy meets another individual or individual canine, they are acquainted with new sights, sounds, and butts to sniff. Taking your little guy to places like the pooch park will furnish him with sufficient chance to connect with his detects. "I now and again take Bruiser to the canine park, which he completely adores! Bruiser always meets new companions there and discovers individuals to sniff and get petted by. This has truly caused him to listen better, less on edge, and genuinely increasingly fulfilled."

6. Give them new toys and pivot out the old ones

You would not have any desire to play with something very similar consistently, would you? At that point, you should not anticipate that your canine should keep on adoring a similar toy that he's had for a considerable length of time. Let him play with a toy for a couple of days and when he becomes exhausted of it, supplant it with another.

"Moogly has such huge numbers of toys yet at the same time gets exhausted. It is crazy! I am continually bringing new toys into the house; however, he has a limited capacity to focus, so they just keep him engaged for some time. We began keeping the entirety of his toys in a canister in the storage room and pivoting them out. He has such a significant number now, and we will switch up to another toy with one that he's had for quite a long time and that he may have disregarded. He adores this, and at whatever point we switch them up, he is similarly as energized as when he gets a spic and span toy." "Katie Adams

Keep Your Dog Mentally and Physically Fit

To be balanced pets, hounds need both mental and physical incitement every day. The longing to "keep occupied" is profoundly imbued in most canines.

Working, chasing, crowding, and guarding breeds are, by all accounts, not the only ones with this need. Indeed, even little types of pooches hold a specific measure of hard-working attitude. For instance, their proprietors realize that these minor folks still appreciate terrier-type practices, for example, pursuing and burrowing. If not given an outlet for their vitality, pups of any size can get dangerous, on edge, or baffled, causing various conduct issues.

Getting Your Puppy The Exercise He Or She Needs

So what amount does practice does your canine genuinely need? There is no definite answer—however, enough exercise to feel worn out. Most solid pooches will profit from practice sessions in both the morning and the night. A safe, fenced region for off-chain practice is perfect, yet on the off chance that you do not approach this, snap a rope on your little guy and take a walk.

Except if your canine has an ailment requiring constrained exercise, at that point make at any rate one of your puppy's trips a vigorous action. Playing with different pooches off-rope in a fenced zone, swimming, playing, or running adjacent to a jogger are altogether unique oxygen-consuming activities. Continuously make sure to watch out for your puppy to look for exhaustion and ensure your pup approaches cold water and shade whenever working out.

A few people even train their mutts to run on a treadmill. You can begin with only a couple of moments, and step by step work up to a brief treadmill practice session. Exercise of this nature will discharge endorphins, which will have a general quieting impact on your puppy's conduct, just as numerous other medical advantages.

Little dog Safe Activities

Exercises appropriate for grown-up canines may not be alright for developing young doggies. Playing is the best decision for a more youthful puppy, regardless of whether it is off-chain with different dogs, playing get, or other games with their human. Set up play dates with companions so your little guy can learn social abilities and get some activity.

Running or biking on asphalt are undependable activities for youthful mutts whose bones are not full-fledged. If you have any inquiries concerning whether a specific sort of activity is alright for your doggy, check with your veterinarian. Continuously check with your veterinarian.

Remember mental incitement! Instructional courses keep a canine's mind sharp, just as they help create and reinforce the bond between dog and human. Abstain from exhausting or dreary exercises. Make it fun! Work on instructing your canine stunts like sit and remain alongside basic spryness works out. Short instructional courses are ideal, mixed with play or rest sessions and bunches of acclaim and love.

Step by step instructions to Tire out a Puppy: 4 Exercises That will Have Him Behaving in No Time

We are pulled in by work (frequently taking a few employments just to make a decent living), family, internet-based life, interests, and ordinarily. We do not set aside a few minutes for our mutts. Indeed, even I work all day with a couple of employments of late! Also, I have high drive hounds that need a great deal of activity.

Mental Stimulation

Tackling riddles and utilizing your psyche is depleting. Try not to trust me? Take a school class or go to a proceeding with instruction class for a day or two.

Get familiar with some new data. What is more, attempt and disclose to me you are not worn out when you are finished! Except if you are utilized to consistently adapting each day. If you need a drained canine, show him something new, or if nothing else, put a turn on the things that he knows by drawing in his brain.

Try not to adhere to the equivalent careful preparing routine with your little guy every day, in a similar exhausting request.

Blend things up, causing him to perform quicker, and make it a game. Mental incitement is likewise pivotal to his joy. Dr. Ian Dunbar (one of my preferred behaviorists) says that psychological exercise tires a pooch physically more than physical exercise does!

That is fantastic stuff! Canines need compliance preparation. They need sports. They need riddles and games. Also, even things to bite on can here and there animate them intellectually. Recollect in past articles, me insinuating not enabling your baby to work out? Presently envision not helping your baby to play or learn or animate his brain. Would you be able to predict it? No books, no toys, next to no verbal collaboration or educating.

That would be brutal. Canines, too, need ever to be invigorated intellectually.

Suppose we do not give it to them through physical and verbal association and learning and compensating excellent conduct. In that case, our puppy will give it to themselves through biting and destroying and yapping and burrowing and bouncing and acting a blockhead. Hyper pooch or high vitality hounds are frequently intellectually more insightful than their partners. They are not satisfied sitting, and playing brings with a couple of toys or chewies.

They ought to be shown in mental activities and games! It does not make a difference what you instruct them:

¢ Fundamental Obedience

¢ Middle of the road Obedience dog games

¢ Propelled Obedience

¢ Dexterity

¢ Motivation Control Games

¢ Stunts

¢ Administration Commands

Or then again, even a handstand up the divider¦

Interestingly, you are instructing and giving that psychological incitement that will fulfill them!

H.I.I.T. Exercise

Have you at any point done H.I.I.T. or High-Intensity Interval Training? Those are four of my most noticeably terrible feared words when they are hung together in a sentence. I am now getting into shape and figuring out how to deadlift, squat, and seat press securely. My fitness coach has faith in H.I.I.T. preparation and draws in me both with weight preparation and cardio a few times each month. I HATE it! I likewise love it because it is justified in that I am getting the results I am looking for, as troublesome as it is.

Also, I rest comfortable thinking about myself!

Your pup can profit as well! I like to take my doggies for high force runs. I sit in a sidelong supine trike and let them pull for a few miles.

More often than not, as long as it is protected, I likewise enable them to establish the tone. Your pooch is a competitor, and he needs the capacity to appreciate work out, REAL exercise! Exercise is additionally useful for his heart and body condition and joints.

Kindly help your canine out and furnish him with some simple exercise every day! His body, his waistline, his circulatory strain, and his mind needs it! The accompanying tips for beginning H.I.I.T. with your puppy are cordiality of SnootyPests.Com.

Start Gently

If you might want to begin H.I.I.T. with your canine, at that point, it is imperative in the first place delicate sessions, mainly if your puppy isn't accustomed to getting a great deal of activity. The ideal approach to do this is to make the eruptions of force shorter, state 10 seconds, and the rest time frames longer, for instance, 40 seconds. As you complete more H.I.I.T. sessions, you will have the option to modify the proportions so that the extraordinary periods are more extended and the rests are shorter.

Try not to Overdo It.

Much like somebody who works out at a recreational center, it is essential to let your pup have rest days to recoup from the extreme exercise. Rest days are similarly as significant as exercise days as they allowed the muscles to assemble and recuperate.

Keep it Short

The extraordinary thing about H.I.I.T. is that it does not require some investment to finish an exercise.

Keep the sessions short, around 10 minutes is sufficient, and make sure to heat up and chill off with some strolling or pull games first.

Make it Fun

You do not need to adhere to running and strolling for your H.I.I.T. session.

Pick exercises your pooch will adore.

On the off chance that they love pursuing balls, at that point, hurl a ball a lofty slope for them for a moment. At that point, walk them for 30 seconds and rehash.

Get imaginative!

Suppose you might want to improve your own and your canine's wellness levels. In that case, high power interim preparation is an unquestionable requirement.

Regular Physical Exercise

I cannot state it enough. Your canine is not outside plotting his activity routine and intending to get fit. A walk around the square or a walk around a couple of miles is not sufficient to tire your pup. Once in a while, I like to appreciate a few mile climbs.

I likewise like urging my pups to swim.

I locate that swimming will deplete my pooches decently fast while strolling and climbing takes numerous long stretches of reliably thorough exercise; swimming is reasonably physically debilitating. My hounds LOVE dock plunging.

You can likewise show your canine to pull loads, pull a truck, and pull a bike or yourself in inline skates (just as skijoring in the day off).

Draw coursing is additionally another fun physical game.

In any case, if strolling is all you are ready to do, do not be disheartened. Fortunately, satisfactory mental incitement is all you need to keep your canine's consideration on you!

You can make things energizing for him with these intellectually animating games to play while strolling him.

The Recall Game

Coming when called is likely THE MOST significant aptitude that you will ever show your canine. Be that as it may, individuals infrequently accept the open the door to take a shot at this while they are on a stroll with their pup on the rope by them! Why not condition the pooch, regularly, that coming when called is a wondrous thing?

So while I am strolling, with my canine in heel position or even toward the finish of the chain (I do not permit any pulling), I start to run in reverse while calling my pup to "come." I make it fun! I skip, I acclaim, and I reward liberally if he reacts rapidly and in a vivified manner. If I need to include more (and I generally do!) I get him to Sit legitimately before me and afterward discover heel once more! Push-Ups

Ahhhhhh, push-ups are one of my preferred activities to engage my puppy's brain and fume his body!

These do not need to be done precisely at home in the middle of my four dividers! I love adding push-ups to a walk for puppy mental incitement.

To begin with, let me clarify: when I state push-ups, I am looking at having my pooch "sit," and afterward "down," and later "sit" in quick progression.

Furthermore, for an incredible video arrangement on the most proficient method to show these essential directions, click here.

To hone my pooch's listening abilities and acquiescence while I am strolling, I direction my canine to "down" (ideally while we are still moving), and afterward, I request various "sits" and "downs" before at last remunerating him with a delectable treat or his preferred toy.

Stowaway and Seek

Find the stowaway is another excellent game to play on a walk or at the recreation center; however, you need two individuals! One individual should shoot away and locate a decent concealing spot. In contrast, the other individual occupies the puppy (or lets him watch first and foremost). At that point, the concealing individual calls the pup to "COME," all while commending him as he attempts to locate his proprietor.

"Fierceness, COME!!!! Great young lady, Good young lady, Good young lady, COME" You can't call once and afterward trust that he is persuaded to discover you. You should laud and spur him until he realizes you!

This is additionally a fun method to set that review or order that we discussed before!

"COME" ought to be F.U.N.! If you reliably work both of the review games, you will see your puppy's review boundlessly improve! Your puppy does not need to be a researcher to mess around while strolling.

Indeed, even the most youthful mutts and young doggies can profit by essentially changing your pace from moderate to quick or too slow. go running with your little dog

Changing pace keeps your canine animated and his emphasis on you!

Circles are additionally fun! Toss around to one side to keep your canine gazing toward you and instruct him to escape your direction. Toss around to one side to propel him to stay aware of a quicker pace.

A great many people scarcely deal with acquiescence while they have their mutts out for a walk.

They aim to go from guide A toward point B and back while they think they are giving their canine exercise. Be that as it may, strolling is not the ideal approach to practice your puppy. Furthermore, incidentally, this is one reason hounds do not tune in to their proprietors while they are out of the house!

Altogether, you should deal with preparing him while you are walking for your canine to hear you out while strolling. Disregard only getting from direct A toward point B "chip away at rope preparing and mess around!

The #1 Way to Physically Exhaust Your Dog?

Put these things together for quick and complete depletion.

My most loved go-to when I need a drained puppy is getting them to perform dutiful directions in a quick-paced way, and afterward, I toss their ball to pursue as a prize.

For example, I get my hurl it and ball (I regularly utilize these because I can toss more remote) and my canine and request various directions; watch me, heel, sit, down, come back to heel, down moving and afterward I mark the finished arrangement of suggestions with a tick or a word and toss the ball the extent that I can for them to recover.

Hounds love to fetch as they quickly come back with the ball (or pull or whatever toy I am utilizing); I choose whether I will request them to drop the toy and afterward toss it once more or demand more compliance before I launch.

I blend it up!

I do not generally request similar practices in succession.

Furthermore, once in a while, I will toss the ball or toy on numerous occasions before returning to acquiescence. Pursuing the toy and recovering is an excellent exercise for my puppies, physically. They are dating and returning as quickly as possible. Once in a while, I also rebound the ball hard or hurl it to get it to give them assortment with their play. On the off chance that I take them out for H.I.I.T., I toss in particular alters, of course, a few downs moving or sits moving and some heel. What is more, when my pups are climbing or returning from swimming, I also request downs from a separation or some fast eye to eye connection and center and behaving so I draw in their brains.

The best incitement comes when you connect all pieces of your canine! The amount Exercise is Too Much for Your Puppy? Try not to utilize tennis balls in little dog preparation.

Would you be able to practice your pup excessively? As per this article from the A.K.C., the appropriate response is more than a basic yes. "We might not have accurate estimations; however, there are a couple of sound judgment contemplations that can assist you with thinking of an arrangement to keep your little dog dynamic and dependable.

First off, think about your canine's breed. A Bulldog little dog and a Border Collie doggy will both love recess. Yet, a Border Collie will most likely have a higher exercise resistance than a Bulldog, also a higher warmth resilience for free airplay.

Breed size issues, as well. Studies show potential connections between an excessive amount of activity and orthopedic ailment in huge breed hounds. Driving your 8-week-old Great Dane for a two-mile walk each day, for example, is likely not a good thought, regardless of whether he could keep up. Many people would not consider taking a little breed pup for a climb that long; however, with higher vitality levels, more giant breeds can trick us into deducing they need more extended strolls than is beneficial for them.

Learn as much about your breed is a decent spot to begin.

Giant and monster breeds develop rapidly and develop gradually, which may mean you need to put off specific exercises, such as hopping in readiness, until they are completely set. the doggy back-and-forth is useful for their teeth and gums.

Then again, toy breeds develop rapidly yet require little visit feedings for the day as doggies, which can mean you may need to change their activity in like manner.

All breeds require mental incitement, however high-drive, working breeds, for example, as Belgian Malinois, Border Collies, and German Shepherd Dogs need more mental stimulation than different species.

No two mutts are similar, yet breed is a central point in deciding movement level. For example, many crowding and working canine breeds will, in general, be very dynamic. These high-vitality hounds need both mental and physical exercise to flourish. On the off chance that they do not have an outlet for their overabundance vitality, they may get ruinous or create different issues. Here are 10 of the most enthusiastic puppies that need a guardian who can stay aware of them.

Tip

Every day strolls alone probably will not be sufficient for some high-vitality hounds. Think about partaking in hound sports, for example, skill or flying circle, to give your canine extra mental and physical incitement.

Easy Ways to Exercise with Your Puppy
01 of 10
Fringe Collie

Fringe collies are incredibly keen, vigorous pooches. They are known for their standard capacities in deftness and plate rivalries. They can make beautiful pets, on the whole, and preeminent, they need a vocation. Their common sense is to crowd; however, they can channel that into pursuing toys or doing riddle games.

Breed Overview

Stature: 18 to 22 inches

WEIGHT: 30 to 55 pounds

PHYSICAL CHARACTERISTICS: Rough or smooth, medium-length coat; can be strong, bicolor, tricolor, merle, or sable; well-adjusted, athletic body

02 of 10

Australian shepherds likewise are profoundly intelligent and cheerful, exceeding expectations in hound sports. They were reared to domesticated group animals, so they will probably search out their own "work" through pursuing creatures or individuals. A few Aussies may act difficult or reserved if not given structure, preparation, and adequate exercise.

Breed Overview

Stature: 18 to 23 inches

WEIGHT: 40 to 65 pounds

PHYSICAL CHARACTERISTICS: Medium-length coat; well-adjusted body; hues incorporate dark, blue merle, red, and red merle

Australian Cattle Dog

Australian dairy cattle hounds are a dedicated, high-vitality breed. A canine with the stamina to group dairy cattle throughout the day can get exhausted as a pet without much of a stretch except if it's given great exercise and mental incitement. Dairy cattle hounds exceed expectations, all things considered, pooch sports and will, in general, appreciate learning stunts and confuse games.

Breed Overview

Stature: 17 to 20 inches

WEIGHT: 30 to 50 pounds

PHYSICAL CHARACTERISTICS: Strong form; smooth twofold coat; hues incorporate blue and red with dark and tan markings

Jack Russell Terrier

Numerous terrier breeds can be exceptionally lively, including Jack Russell terriers. These little canines indeed are not languid lap hounds. Without preparing and overwhelming day by day work out, they may channel their abundance vitality into burrowing, yapping, and other bothersome practices. They regularly do well in learning hound sports and different stunts.

Breed Overview

Tallness: 13 to 14 inches

WEIGHT: 13 to 17 pounds

PHYSICAL CHARACTERISTICS: Smooth or broken coat; hues incorporate white with dark, brown, or tan markings

05 of 10

Weimaraner

The Weimaraner was reared for chasing and keeps on having that drive to be moving, running long separations. These mutts will, in general, be cordial and warm; however, some can be hyperactive. Without organized preparation and a colossal measure of activity every day, Weimaraners can get focused or ruinous.

Breed Overview

Stature: 23 to 27 inches

The Belgian Malinois regularly works for law implementation, and it needs some sort of employment to flourish. If you pick a Malinois as a pet, let your puppy generally be interested in hound sports. Notwithstanding adequate daily physical exercise, nose work, and the following are incredible choices for mental incitement.

18 of the Easiest Puppy Breeds to Train

Owning a canine accompanies a great deal of obligation. Canines need a protected domain and a nutritious eating regimen. They need veterinary consideration. Furthermore, they need exercise, care, and a lot of preparation. It is no big surprise that notwithstanding scanning for a canine who is anything but difficult to possess, numerous individuals need a puppy who will effectively adopt new deceives (or figure out how to calm himself outside).

Honestly, despite everything, you will have to invest a lot of energy preparing your canine. What are more, hounds that are anything but difficult to train regularly still need loads of your time and vitality? Yet, the puppies who are most effortless to prepare will rapidly connect directions with activities. What is more, they will need to satisfy you and adhere to your guidelines more often than not.

Look at the charming canine breeds that have a substantial possibility of rapidly realizing what you instruct them.

1. Bernese mountain hound

The Bernese mountain hound is a well-disposed breed that takes to preparing effectively. As per the A.K.C., this "delicate goliath" is mellow tempered and adores open air exercises. This breed needs a moderate degree of activity, which will, as a rule, prevent your canine from yelping or carrying on.

The Bernese Mountain Dog Club reports that "with the preparation basic for responsibility for the huge working breed, Berners are commonly delicate, accommodating, and tolerant." But they do require a lot of association with individuals. Furthermore, the club prompts preparing should consistently utilize positive systems.

Next: A satisfying human-canine who wants to joke around 2.

Havanese

Havanese little dog running in the grass with a ball.

The Havanese consistently needs to satisfy his proprietor. That implies he adores adapting new directions and stunts. The A.K.C. reports the "Havanese are keen, trainable, and normal comedians." This pooch breed is a decent decision for fledgling canine proprietors. Be that as it may, remember he needs organization and adores being the focal point of consideration. As indicated by the Havanese Club of America, the significant worry with a Havanese little dog "is to give adequate socialization to the puppy so as to become an active member of society both in the home and the network. This normally includes an introduction to plenty of others and different mutts."

Next: A keen canine who needs to utilize his vitality satisfying his proprietor

2. Outskirt collie little dog

In case you are an accomplished pooch proprietor and just need a canine that will take to preparing admirably, you should think about an outskirt collie. The fringe collie has vast amounts of vitality yet needs to satisfy you. The A.K.C. preaches, "The uncanny knowledge, physicality, and trainability of outskirt collies have an ideal outlet in nimbleness work." Translation?

This compulsive worker canine will never be a habitual slouch. So you will have to use your very own portion vitality keeping him occupied.

The Border Collie Society of America reports you will likewise need to set aside a few minutes for progressing preparing "in dutifulness, submission, compliance!" Activities, for example, agility, Flyball, Rally, crowding, and following, all empower your canine to adopt new mental abilities. Furthermore, they can help you give your outskirt collie the incredible day-by-day practice he needs.

Next: A spunky little canine who is snappy to learn 4. Small schnauzer

3.   Small schnauzer lying on the grass

The small schnauzer thinks that it is simple to adopt new directions. Be that as it may, you will unquestionably to work to keep this high-vitality hound involved. Also, you will need to prepare him not to bark too much. Luckily, the A.K.C. clarifies, "This breed hungers for human friendship, which, joined with the breed's knowledge, makes him simple to prepare for a wide range of exercises. He is alert and spunky, yet besides faithful to directions." The American Miniature Schnauzer Club reports the breed profits by essential compliance preparation and continuous socialization. Be that as it may, they are "submissive and snappy to adapt, amazingly committed, fun-loving, and exceptionally tender."

Next: A shockingly laid-back" and trainable" terrier

4. Fringe terrier

Two fringe terriers in the day off

The fringe terrier is frequently viewed as an exceptionally trainable pooch. What is more, he's laid-back for a terrier" however, do not imagine that implies he won't require a great deal of movement. The A.K.C. clarifies the outskirt terrier is "depicted as 'rock solid when working, however at home, they All dogs deserve good care and do not have to be arduous or costly to train the puppy. If you are sharing your house with a new puppy or an elderly dog, it's never too early to continue your dog training. Most dogs are happy with the stability and trust that comes from teaching.

Dogs want more than anything to make their owners happy that's why they train efficiently. Before starti, make a list of the basic commands you want to teach: "Sitting," "still," "come," "down," or "no" (always useful commands). You can also control the king, teach them not to order food, and avoid the house's accidents. All this can be done-you need consistency, praise, occasional rewards, a lot of patience, and positivism.

Be cautious and forward-looking in the event of an accident while teaching a dog to go to the bathroom. This is one of your dog's most important things to teach, starting with a program. Hogs are typical animals, so take them to the toilet after feeding, playing, waking up from a nap, before going to bed, or looking for a place to urinate and add these moments into the system.

When the dog is in the right place, laud him a lot. Next time only snacks are going to be motivated. The puppy will learn when and when to do that as time goes on. Remember, it is not all perfect puppies.

When you first start focusing on dog training, it can feel daunting. If you are uncertain where to get going, create a week-by-week plan to organize yourself better. Select one or two key commands every week to focus on. Prepare to make any changes to the dog's lifestyle to avoid or change issues with behavior are acceptable tempered, friendly, and trainable." With a lot of activity, they can live similarly as cheerfully in the city as in the nation. As indicated by the Border Terrier Club of America, the outskirt terrier needs to satisfy you. "This makes it simple to prepare essential house habits, for example, housebreaking, strolling on a rope, disregarding trash, disregarding garments and children's toys, not hopping on individuals or furniture, sitting and staying, and coming when called (excepting the nearness of a squirrel or hare)."

Next: A peppy and perky mutts who take orders from you or your children

5. Fighter

The fighter is an insightful and calm canine who adapts to new directions effectively. As indicated by the A.K.C., these exceptionally dynamic pooches "appreciate physical and mental difficulties." But they are additionally "perky and fun-loving. Their understanding and defensive nature have earned them notoriety for being an incredible pooch for youngsters."

The American Boxer Club reports; however, numerous fighters prevail at execution occasions. The "same natural insight that makes him brisk to adapt likewise gives the fighter his very own brain." The club adds that a coach needs to remain "deliberate and quiet."

6. Doberman pinscher

Just experienced pooch proprietors ought to think about a Doberman pinscher. If you are ready to give predictable preparation and initiative, he can turn into an agreeable individual from your family. Recall Dobermans, in the same way as other different canines, can get ruinous and forceful if you let them become exhausted continuously or forlorn.

As indicated by the A.K.C., the Doberman who is all around prepared and mingled "is a caring pet, a world-class family gatekeeper, [and] a flexible canine competitor." The Doberman Pinscher Club of America reports these pooches to require canny taking care of yet are adaptable in exercises, including search and salvage, surrender, and work as a guide or treatment hound.

7. German shepherd

The German shepherd is anxious to please and prepared to work. What is more, as the A.K.C. reports, this extremely dynamic breed needs routine mental and physical exercise. In any case, fans love the breed for its reliability, fearlessness, and "the capacity to learn and hold directions for a stunning number of particular occupations."

The German Shepherd Dog Club of America reports straightforward preparation should start the minute your doggy shows up home. A German shepherd doggy can get familiar with his name and essential directions as ahead of schedule as about two months old.

Next: A canine who is intelligent and bossy, however, takes well to prepare.

8. Pembroke Welsh corgi

The Pembroke Welsh corgi is a little functioning canine who cherishes having a vocation to do. The A.K.C. clarifies, "The

Pembroke reacts well to preparing and adores his family; however, he may attempt to group you." Corgis (and corgi proprietors) advantage from acquiescence classes. What's more, the A.K.C. guarantees, "The time you spend in preparing, particularly during the principal year of your pet's life, will be reimbursed many occasions over by giving you a polite buddy, one that is attached to you and your family for an amazing remainder."

The Pembroke Welsh Corgi Club of America that corgis "are astute canines, trainable and great with kids." Nonetheless, "this breed is splendid and bossy" if you aren't in control, they will cheerfully accept the job, and an issue is a lot harder to address than forestall."

9. Brilliant retriever

The brilliant retriever makes an incredible ally for beginner hound proprietors. This canine needs to please. What is more, as the A.K.C. notes, "They have a blissful, fun-loving way to deal with life and keep up this uncorrupt conduct for longer than some different breeds."

As indicated by the Golden Retriever Club of America, hounds" including brilliant retrievers" are issue solvers and learn by experimentation. Yet, your bright isn't the one in particular who will get the hang of during the way toward preparing. "As you show your canine the means important to get familiar with the acquiescence works out, he will react effectively or erroneously, and you should figure out how to react suitably," the club says.

Next: A very famous breed that cherishes individuals and different pooches

10. Labrador retriever

The Labrador retriever accepts the cake as the most famous pup in the U.S." and all things considered. The breed is anything but difficult to prepare, regardless of whether you need one as a family pooch or working canine. The A.K.C. reports Labs to mingle well with people and with different pups. Be that as it may, you shouldn't "confound his laid-back character for low vitality. The Labrador retriever is very dynamic" he is never met a terrace he didn't care for." According to the Labrador Retriever Club, these canines are "anxious to please and non-forceful toward man or creature."

Next: A savvy and enthusiastic laborer that is anxious to please

11. Australian shepherd

The Australian shepherd can get the hang of anything you can instruct him. Be that as it may, you have to keep him occupied and engaged. You will presumably need to continually devise new games and difficulties for this profoundly intelligent canine. As the American Kennel Club clarifies, this current breed's "solid work drive can make Aussies more pooch than an inactive pet proprietor may expect. Aussies are astoundingly astute, very equipped for outflanking a clueless beginner proprietor."

The United States Australian Shepherd Association reports these canines are exceptionally trainable and "effectively housebroken because they are clever and anxious to please." But you will have to channel your puppy's vitality to monitor his conduct.

Next: A terrier with an exceptionally cheerful demeanor 13. Norwich terrier

The Norwich terrier is vigorous and needs a ton of action. Be that as it may, he is anything but difficult to prepare, and even amateur canine proprietors will have the option to deal with him. The A.K.C. reports the Norwich terrier needs both physical and mental exercise. In any case, these puppies make "savvy, willing allies and can exceed expectations in an assortment of canine exercises."

The Norwich Terrier Club of America clarifies, however, the breed initially filled in as a working terrier; these mutts "were likewise esteemed for their amiable demeanor." Today, "the breed holds its unique chasing senses, little size, and joyful disposition so prized by early huntsmen on the two sides of the Atlantic."

12. Papillon

The papillon is another canine who will effectively adopt new deceives however needs you to keep him involved. The A.K.C.

reports this "dynamic" hound breed likes to exercise and takes to prepare. Their insight assumes a job in their trainability. However, "it causes that they like to please and be with those they love."

The Papillon Club of America clarifies these canines are "cheerful, alarm, and inviting," however you should be a steady coach to draw out the best in your puppy. "Predictable, committed mentors thoroughly enjoy the inclination this breed has for pretty much anything. Yet, this is a breed that gains from every experience, and a conflicting mentor will not deliver steady outcomes" even with fundamental aptitudes like housebreaking."

13. Brussels griffon

The Brussels griffon reliably positions as probably the most effortless canine to prepare. As the A.K.C. notes, they are "social, amicable, and effectively prepared and will typically coexist well with other family pets and respectful youngsters." Just remember they are one of the more high-upkeep hound breeds since they want to remain nearby to their proprietors and do not care for being disregarded.

In any case, the American Brussels Griffon Association reports this breed "exceeds expectations in compliance (the show ring), submission, dexterity, rally preliminaries, following tests, and as treatment hounds."

14. Poodle

The standard poodle reliably positions as one of the most astute and respectful breeds," which can, at times, feel like a phenomenal mix. The A.K.C. guarantees, "Poodles are insightful and effectively prepared to do various things. A portion of the exercises that poodles appreciate is following, chasing, nimbleness, and acquiescence."

The Poodle Club of America encourages that "a poodle ought to be an individual from the family. Forthcoming proprietors of poodles ought to be prepared to give a fenced-in region in which the poodle can work out, or be set up to walk the poodle normally on a chain."

17. Rottweiler

The Rottweiler takes effectively to prepare; however, he unquestionably needs work to keep him glad. As indicated by the A.K.C., this current pooch's "insight, perseverance, and readiness to work make him reasonable as a police hound, herder, administration hound, treatment hound, compliance contender, and a dedicated friend." You will have to prepare him on fundamental dutiful directions, just as social aptitudes. What is more, you will additionally need to outfit his regular regional senses. As the A.K.C. puts it, "He needs to realize that you are in control, regardless of whether he is twice your size."

The American Rottweiler Club clarifies these mutts "need socialization, practice and animating mental difficulties. With these things, you will have a great partner; without them, your Rottweiler may get ruinous and crazy."

15. Shetland sheepdog

The Shetland sheepdog is a little yet extremely dynamic pooch that reliably performs well in agility and other canine games," a demonstration of his capacity to learn. As per the A.K.C., you should take advantage of the breed's grouping legacy with "task-based exercise." The American Shetland Sheepdog Association clarifies these canines "want to satisfy their proprietors and a colossal limit regarding love and friendship." Additionally, "the Sheltie is uncommonly trainable and responsive, in addition to being a remarkable laborer in submission, grouping, and readiness preliminaries."

Chapter Four: Family Training

It is not just something to be left up to the parents of the house to show proper behavior to your puppy. While mom and dad will typically assume the most responsibilities for the training of the family dog, it is still important to engage kids in the process.

You need to know that it must respond and behave politely for all members of the family. Plus, allowing the kids to help with their dogs' education can be a wonderful learning experience for them. Being involved in training a dog can teach children patience and compassion - and succeeding at the task will promote positive self-esteem.

Dogs normally do not see kids as sources of power, but when kids want to follow them, any teaching methods that focus on physical corrections appear to backfire. Using reward-based teaching strategies like lure-and-reward or clicker training approaches, children are typically more effective. As most dogs work well to win food, games, and other fun prizes, this is well for all.

Any family member can participate in training, feeding, and grooming your dog – ensure they are doing the job. In order to keep them on track, most children under ten (and some older children, too) require constant monitoring and parental help.

Do not expect more engagement than your child is adequately mature to provide and continue to verify regularly that their tasks have been done-the protection and security of your pet are at stake.
Yeah, kids must practice honesty, but this can never come at the cost of the well-being of animals.

Before adding young co-trainers, it's typically better for an adult to initiate every new lesson for the puppy. The dog has a basic knowledge of what to do in that way, and the kids need not start from scratch. This way, teaching will go more smoothly, and the children will feel less stress and immense success.
To get kids involved in your dog's training, first, let them watch you working with the dog, then show them how to do it themselves. Stand by, at least in the beginning, to coach and support – and to get the lesson back on track, if necessary.

Some children turn out to be better trainers than many adults. If your child is one of these marvels, celebrate this success by allowing him or her to take on more of the training and teach the dog new tricks and tasks. Many positive dog trainers now encourage children to participate in their obedience classes fully, so check around. There may be one that you, your dog, and your kids can attend together.

Having dog training a family affair for everyone is an enjoyable and satisfying experience. To continue, you must commit to declaring the rules that will control the actions of your dog, and let everybody know that these rules must be enforced by everyone - so continuity in the family is key to producing successful training results.

Establishing The Rules

Be sure everyone in your family and your dog learns and follows the same rules; otherwise, your best-laid training plans will crumble. If one person allows the dog to jump on them or play rough games, for example, your dog will try these behaviors with other people. And when your family isn't consistent about keeping the rules, do not expect your dog to either!

The best time to establish rules is before you bring your puppy or adult dog home. That way, everyone can be consistent right from the start. However, chances are pretty good that if you are reading this article now, you probably already have your dog at home with you. For this cause, what needs to be done is to start immediately. – establish your "good dog rules" today, make sure the whole family knows what they are, and have everyone agree to follow them, starting immediately.

Family Meeting Time

Call the whole family together to create a list of the essential rules regarding the dog. Encourage each person, including the children, to offer ideas and describe how they would like the dog to behave so everyone will feel included.

Discuss the reasons for each rule you decide to implement, so its importance is understood. Significant rules – such as not feeding on the table or the types of play that will be allowed – must be the same for everyone.

Write down your list of agreed-upon rules and let the children illustrate the page by drawing pictures of your dog is okay. The more personal involvement each family member has with the list of dog rules, the more likely everyone will be to abide by them. When your list is finished and illustrated, please post it in a central location, such as the refrigerator, so no one forgets the rules (or pretends to).

I cannot stress enough just how important it is for your children (and everyone else in the house) to have the same mindset and understanding of how you want your dog handled during training.

Dogs do not come into the world learning polite etiquette, so do not ask the family member to abide by laws it does not yet recognize. Training is a process that involves practice and time. To keep your dog out of trouble while it is learning how to act correctly, both management and preparation would be important.

You will also need to find ways to discourage your dog from engaging in negative activities that could turn into bad habits when teaching your proper dog manners. If you let the house run wild of your untrained puppy, it will potty in all the wrong places, chew your things, snatch unwatched food from tables and counters, tear down doors, dig holes in the garden of roses, and maybe head down the lane. Before they are shown more fitting acts, dogs know little better than to do these things.

Begin by restricting the access of your dog to places where it might be misbehaving secretly. Do not let him have the absolute run of your house until he's completely home-trained and has mastered when to chew and when not to chew. Hold your dog in the same room you are in, so you can keep an eye on it and stop dirty, risky, expensive mistakes.

A proactive approach will allow your dog to get used to your general household routine and to practice the good behaviors you are teaching it. If the dog tries to slip away when you get distracted, either block the room's doorways with baby gates or leash your dog to your belt to keep it with you. When no one is available to keep an eye on the dog, confine it in an enclosed puppy-proofed area either indoors or outdoors.

Keep Training Consistent

Training can be fun and fulfilling for the entire family, or it can be fraught with frustration. Which way it goes depends upon how consistently you and your family keep the dog on track. The best way to be consistent is to decide on a set of rules everyone in the family can follow and get the family positively involved in your dog's training.

Raising a great canine family companion is not a job for just one person. It takes a village – or at least a cooperative family – to raise and train a well-behaved dog. Family-oriented games to help your dog learn simple commands and good manners. And make sure to supervise any play involving kids, please.

Thank You - Take It

When asked happily, this game will teach your dog to release items from its mouth. Any item in which you begin to teach this should be big enough for your dog to grasp one end while holding the other. It works well with a length of thick, soft knotted rope or a big, durable stuffed plush toy.

To make it fun, begin by wiggling the toy. Tell "take it in a playful voice and encourage your pup to catch on. Praise and encourage the dog, as you keep the other end, to chew and play with the toy. Tell "thank you" after a few moments and give a treat from the other hand to your puppy, keeping it about six inches away from the side of his muzzle. To get the reward, the dog will see and scent the treat and will let go of the toy.

Do not take the toy; keep keeping it." Compliment him for having it and let it play for a few minutes before saying thank you. "Compliment him for having it and let it play for a few minutes before you say thank you again and trade it for another treat.

Do not pick up a toy; keep having it. " Compliment him for having it and let it play for a few minutes before saying thank you. "Compliment him for having it and let it play for a few minutes before you say thank you again and trade it for another treat.

Many dogs are automatically released, awaiting a reward. If it is, applaud the toy with a playful flourish and give it back quickly, saying take it. The toy itself and the pleasure of grabbing and playing with it becomes a treat.

Chapter five: Dogs and barking problems

To drive someone mad, barking nonstop is enough.

Any living thing your dog sees outside the window, like vehicles, persons, even objects.

If one item disappears from the viewpoint of your puppy, another one reappears, and it goes on and on. Most of us get so annoyed when we end up yelling at our dog to get him to calm down. This technique, unfortunately, brings more excitement to the high fear levels of your puppy.

Your dog's mind reveals that you feel the same way by barking at him, and now you have nothing but a noisy circus going on as you are trying to focus on the lane.

The good news is that you can slowly diminish your dog's incessant barking with a little training and some patience when you are out. These are some tips to help you solve the problem:

1. For beginners, try being a role model if you want your dog to be more comfortable and laid back.

Whenever your dog gets nervous, play some soft music, and keep calm and collected. He caresses his head slowly and listens to him soothingly as he barks. You would be shocked by how easily your dog or puppy turns his head toward you to receive some of the affection, and without the barking, of course.

2. There is nothing wrong with bringing a small water bottle for a more drastic conditioning method with which you can squirt your dog any time he decides to bark excessively. Some puppies and dogs dislike being sprayed on them with a short blast of spray. Usually, whatever it is they are doing, they will immediately leave. And be sure to give a firm command at the same time you spray your pet. You can eventually replace the water bottle with this command because your dog will associate it with the same shocking experience of being squirted with water.

3. Try using a crate. A straightforward solution is to use a box that your dog can sit in whenever you need to drive somewhere with him. The container should be visually limited so that your dog does not get stimulated by all of the action he can see out of the window. This in itself is enough to keep your dog from barking excessively. Of course, this may not be easy if you have a large dog. However, using a crate is a perfect way to keep small to medium-sized dogs quiet while you are on the road.

How To Treat A Dog That Barks For Care?

Handling all the loud barking of a new puppy can be such a terrifying activity for any new dog owner.

The majority of prospective dog owners are not prepared for the extreme amount of barking and yelping that young puppies tend to do the minute they arrive in their new home.

While it is expected, some puppies, especially at night,

do not allow their owners the luxury of calming down.

The fear of being left alone is one of the most critical stages that a puppy can go through.

Except in the sense of you leaving the house, I am not talking about being alone.

Even when you leave the room for a split second, individual dogs can go crazy.

They cannot stand alone, and they are used to seeing their mommy or nonstop littermates.

What do you do when presented with this scenario?

If any time he screams, you rush to your puppy to soothe and caress him, then you are only feeding the habit and making a lazy dog.

On the other hand, if you ignore him and let him bark his brains out, you will be very angry with the rest of the family (especially your spouse) to allow the barking to occur.

It is like getting trapped between a hard spot and a rock.
We do, though, have some ideas to help you cope with the case with your puppy barking:

1. The first step is to try to ignore your puppy's barking if at all possible without yelling at him. Yelling will either scare him from wanting to come near you or further add to his anxiety levels that and he will continue barking.
2. A product called "teaching lead" will encourage your puppy to be in the house at all times around you. When he is getting used to his freedom, use specific sorts of resources to be around you.
3. Try refraining from long and drawn out exits as you leave the house.

While it is understandable to want to pet your puppy before leaving the house to speak to her sweetly, it just causes more tension because she will continue to equate your actions with leaving her side with you.
When you get in, the same suggestion goes.
After stepping through the entrance, stop central and thrilling welcomes.

4.	To get your dog to calm down automatically while she is barking, consider using an essential teaching assist. The best idea is a water bottle that sends a short blast of streaming spray. Or you can use a little tin filled with a pair of pennies in it. As soon as you leave her side, and she begins to bark, throw the can into her field. It will make a disturbing noise while diverting her focus at the same time.

Chapter six: Dog's behaviour

When these timid puppies grow up in nearly any situation they come into, they will become particularly needy and turn to their parents for reinforcement. And sadly, while "run to mommy or daddy" is essential any time she gets afraid if she does not get the calming treatment needed, your dog can begin to initiate violence. This may be classified as fear-induced violence.

Ironically enough, you just perpetuate the action if you always caress and soothe your dog as she shows intense shyness and becomes scared.

I understand that when she needs you, it is hard to imagine avoiding your timid and frightened puppy, so if you want to change her

behavior and make the dog become a brave and social animal, you are going to have to avoid letting her know that being afraid is "okay."

Helping Your Shy Puppy Change

If your dog displays symptoms of anxiety and timidity early on when you try to help her adapt, and you will have to be careful.

It would be better to coax the dog to know you are no longer going to be her guardian.

Behaviors she is used to doing when she gets frightened may have to be avoided, such as barking when she is surprised between her knees, darting around if she sees a regular part of the outside, such as a human walking or a bush swinging by the wind, etc.

Some of the advice you can use to help your puppy become less shy are:

1. Help your family and friends to ignore your puppy's fear-induced barking or cry each time they want to pet him. Up until this point, anytime anyone arrives, your dog has behaved out of fear, and when these people instinctively interrupt the tactic, your dog has discovered that this action works in her favor. Your dog will, however, begin to realize that fear-induced barking will no longer work as long as your friends and family support your desires for training.

2. Whenever you expect people to come to your house, make sure to have your puppy tight by a leash. Take your dog with you as you approach the guests if you can allow the dog to be with you at every time. The difference from now on is that when it starts crying, barking, or hiding behind your legs, you will now act confidently without petting or soothing her. This will help your dog become braver while teaching her that her old behavior will not work anymore.

Chewing & Nipping: How To Stop Your Puppy from these 2 Annoying Behaviors

People also adore them even when they act out in destructive ways with annoying habits, especially when they are cute and well.

However, these bad practices are based on our expectations of how they ought to behave.

They are just behaving like - well - dogs to our puppies!

But they must learn to act in the human world to keep the home a secure and peaceful environment, and it is our duty as their owners to make that possible.

With an accurate training program, any puppy can learn to stop unpleasant habits like:

Nipping: Nipping during playtime, mainly when they get excited, is typical for all puppies.

But no matter how right your puppy is or how innocent it may seem, nipping is a bad habit that must be immediately stopped immediately.

Your puppy has to understand that his teeth do not touch human skin, except in play. Curbing this activity now will significantly minimize the risk of your puppy growing up and biting you in the future.

Transform his biting habit into relying on his toys instead of your hands as your dog tries to nip.

Have toys like chewy, rubber toys that welcome his mouth, especially those that come with treats inside, and fluffy, colorful plush toys that will pique his attention.

Before you start teaching him, you do not have to wait for your puppy to grow bigger. And puppies of 8 weeks old will come to recognize that nipping is not tolerated.

Tell "ouch" and back up for a couple of seconds as he tries to bite during play.

If he tries to bite again, walk out, go to another room, and lock the door, but do not leave him alone for more than a minute.

Leaving him and going with the door shut to another room shows him that biting hard "makes the fun go away." He will finally learn to regulate his nipping pressure.

When he knows how to gently nip, lift the bar, and say "ouch" to the soft bites before he learns to avoid absolutely at the edge.

Chewing: Another irritating behavior that frustrates us dog owners is when these adorable little animals chew on our things (especially those brand new shoes). Puppies have an insatiable need to chew, mainly when they go through their teething period, to soothe their aching gums.

Stopping your dog from trying to relieve his suffering would be unfair so that you may divert his chewing to his toys rather than your shoes, clothing, reviews, and so on.

Always have tons of toys available for him to chew on. Get him used to gnaw on these toys by having them around with him at all times while he's still a tiny puppy. Be sure to locate these items in a confined area with your puppy to focus his attention on other stuff around the house; tell "no chew" if you see him chewing on something he's not supposed to, then immediately swap the object with his chewing toy.

When he starts chewing on his doll, make sure to encourage him.

Chapter seven: When your dog chases cars

Because no two dogs are exactly alike in personality and temperament, neither can there be just a single method to accomplish all dogs' educational lessons. Your dog may respond to only one particular form, and he may get the message quickly. You may have to use several methods, and the schooling may take up to four days because it takes the average dog approximately four to five days to learn the middle thing.

An important key is consistency. Consistency here doesn't mean selecting one method and sticking to it; instead, the texture is desired. Each instance of car chasing must culminate an unpleasant consequence that the dog must relate to his action of chasing the car.

You can't run out the door, after the fact, or even during the actual chasing, call your dog to you and beat him senseless, and expect them to learn anything. If that type of action resulted in learning, it would merely be his response in your command "come" would result in getting his brains knocked in. The dog must relate the consequences to the act of car chasing, and nothing else!

Tackling this problem will require time, effort, and perhaps some creativity on your part. Suppose you truly love your dog and are concerned for his safety, the safety of others, and your liability. In that case, you will devote the next four to five days to the task of convincing your dog that car chasing always will conclude in an unpleasant consequence.

Day 1

Tie a length of clothesline rope to your dog's standard slip-chain training collar. About 35 feet of line will do just fine. Allow the dog to drag the bar around the yard. Position yourself close to the end of the dragging line to wait for your "opportunity."
Act relaxed, but keep one eye on the dog and the other on the end of that line. Please do not give any attention to your dog, so when an automobile approaches, watch for the moment he starts his barking charge. You want your dog's attention focused entirely on the car during that specific moment.

When that moment has arrived, please pick up the end of the line and jerk it as much as you can, giving it everything you've got. This jerk should put a shock into your dog as he is stopped in mid-air. Pull the line and when your dog is at your feet, give the animal an abrupt shaking, enough to provide him with the message. Verbally shock him as well, with loud, angry words, showing your complete and total displeasure.

The preceding procedure must be fast accomplished. Remember, the dog must relate this displeasing series of events with his act of chasing the car. If you are too slow to jerk the line, then the dog's mind will sidetrack to something else. And just as the pool's timing is essential, so is the importance of your verbal assault, ensuring that he knows you are unhappy with his decision to chase the car.

During the second day of training your pet not to chase cars and other moving objects, the same exact sequence should be repeated as day one – with the dog dragging the thirty-five-foot chord. In each instance, an automobile passes without the dog yielding to temptation, and he earns your price; a genuine, enthusiastic price!

If he senses that you are going to the bar and violates the order, you have to follow him through with the series, almost as if he had been through the chase behavior all the way.

Any dogwise enough to feel a correction approaching, and change his behavior accordingly, will soon play a "catch me if you can." game.

Your dog must know that any mistake, even the minor, immediately brings the full force of the correction.

Day 3

When the third day comes around, your dog will be getting the idea that you do not want him to chase cars, that his actions displease you so much and drive you mad.

So far, you have made the first approach in scholarly communication.

You must extend this training to the third day to include the car as an object of disappointment and relate this to your disappointment.

On the third day, you will need help from a friend or neighbor who will volunteer to drive their vehicle.

You will require a few more teaching aids as well.

Along with an empty aluminum, soda can come with around ten or so pennies inside and maybe a few water balloons, three or four tin cans bound together on a cord should be in the front seat next to the driver. When you go indoors and out of reach, encourage your dog to pull the line across the yard.

Watch your pet from a secret viewing point.

When the dog charges the truck, the driver can without slowing down) let go of the tin cans. You do not want the dog to be struck by the cans, but more to confuse the animal with noisy clinking sounds.

This action is followed immediately by you, the dog owner, emerging from your place of concealment, grabbing the line, and reeling the dog in for a good shaking and verbal chewing out.

The driver rounds the block in the meantime, and you can retire into the building, leaving the dog alone for the next car pass.
You should emerge happily and give the dog an over-abundance of encouragement on the second pass and any subsequent pass where the dog does not threaten to charge the vehicle. The driver can encourage another surprising training assist
if the dog chooses to charge the vehicle.
All that is required should be four or five such passes.
Even if the dog continues running but aborts the aim before it gets close enough for the driver to let go of the tin cans or water balloons, you have to jump out of the house, take the line, and chew the dog out again verbally.

If he changes his mind in the midst of the
charge, you might be wondering whether the dog should be corrected. Things are either black or white in the eyes of a puppy. In between, there are no grey zones.
An owner who can surrender unconditionally is to a dog and an owner who is willing to negotiate.
Therefore, with any overt action towards moving vehicles, the dog must be corrected so that he finally begins to understand the need to avoid the vehicle entirely.

Car Chasing No More: Day 4 (Final Training Day)

This is the day of the final exam and graduation!

Cut the long line in two, and allow the dog to drag about 15 feet of cable. Have a family member release the dog in the front yard, still carrying his line.

If you were to put yourself in the back seat of your assistant's vehicle, it would help.

To persuade you that your dog has kicked the drug is now reformed, and sees cars with utter disdain, have your driver making as many passes as is required.

The most hardheaded, stubborn dog, who views the short line, and your absence is in for quite a surprise as a reason to go charging. At his charge, your driver must stop the car. The shock of you emerging from the vehicle will shock the dog even more than before. Get the line now, jerk your disobedient dog towards you, make sure his two front feet leave the ground and keep airborne while you carry out the loudest physical attack you ever gave him.

Lay this disobedient chewing into the dog; make it count!

Remember that this could mean life or death for your dog in the future, so do not feel bad about laying your anger into him to communicate through the animal's mind.

Keep in mind that there will be nothing else as compromise. In fact, our dog will either associate this experience with displeasure or not. You must make sure that it is as displeasing as humanely possible. Send the dog scampering back into his yard as you get back into the car and drive away.

A Final Word For All Of The "Humanitarians"

Let us warn you that we are teaching your dog to escape a bloody, excruciating, flesh-tearing death, for the humanitarians who would gasp and raise the accusing finger at this alleged "inhumane way of training a dog. And note that the dog will always be a suspect, the drivers of the vehicle will be stunned, and the dog's owner will always be the culprit.

A couple days of jerking your dog by the line, crying and shouting, and using shock treatment to establish the connection of disappointment with a driving vehicle is nothing compared to your family dog lying on the streets for hours with broken limbs, ripped skin, mangled body parts, all the while motorists move in the world without caring until eventually, someone slows, only to be too late as your doggie leaves this world.

Isn't your dog worth it?

Dog chasing cars: Why Do Dogs Risk Death With The "Thrill Of The Chase"?

The brakes squeal, the car swerves, and the inevitable THUD of wheel meeting dogs are followed by the crash of the careening, out-of-control automobile. The victims? The dog, of course. The occupants, presumably. But who was the fault? The owner of the dog.

If technically liable or not, the blame for the conduct of the dog lies squarely on the ì the dog owner, just as a father is responsible for his child's actions.

There are many reasons for such offensive behaviors in our dogs. But the main reason is simply the thrill of the chase. The instinct is strong in canines. Many mothers have warned their children that "never run from a dog" because it triggers an automatic drive in the dog to pursue, overcome, and emerge victoriously.

The feral canine ran down his prey.

Nature gave him this instinct and the speed to carry out the challenge. Chasing games in the wild was a severe enterprise and a survival condition.

And, of course, the excitement of the chase was still there.

The domesticated dog no longer has to hunt the prey for safety, but a part of his instinct is still the joy of pursuit.

With sports dogs on the track, man capitalizes on the impulse.

By making them' race dogs,' chasing a mechanical bunny, man abuses greyhounds' instinct.

And through the jungle, fighting tracking dogs pursue an unknown enemy.

In specific ways, instinctive protectiveness is blamed for dogs attacking cars.

They chase just the cars that approach "their territory." Contact is what is required here.

It might be pretty straightforward if we could all sit down over a cup of coffee with our dogs and say something like, "Look buddy, we have a problem here, but it doesn't work like that, sadly.

And even though your dog listens to your "NO" or "STOP" verbal order when he sees a driving vehicle, he's still going to dash for it.

The Excitement Minimization

A way must be found to reduce the thrill and emphasize the disastrous consequences of chasing moving vehicles. While the chase's joy is spontaneous and never can be entirely erased, it can be minimized and made less important than the behavior's consequences.

Most dogs understand how to avoid conditions where a bad encounter may be related to the situation.

However, for individual dogs who have been struck by cars and have survived, they will usually not hold the experience.

This is because the trauma of being hit by a vehicle is typically so immediate and so intense that the dog does not attribute the pain to the vehicle or its actions before the chase.

But mother nature has implanted something else along with the instinct to chase, the dog's capacity to understand through association.

Through associating his acts with satisfying or displeasing consequences, he can understand.

If you have trained your dog effectively to let him know that cars and motorcycles are deadly, it will help.

Chapter Eight: Dealing With Dogs' Separation And Anxiety

In order to help your dog feeling more secure when you are away, for the fastest results possible, use the following tips:

1. It is an exciting feeling to see a young puppy or a new adult dog. It is so easy to give lots of love and affection to the newest member of the family. But spending all your time with your new dog can have adverse effects, especially when you return to your everyday life where you are out of the house all day.

Give a lot of love to your new puppy, but still, let him get used to being alone even while you are at home.

It can progressively get him used to your absence because it does not cause a painful encounter.

Start by going to another room and shutting the door behind you, leaving your dog in a new position on its own.

Do this several times a day.

Then, leave him in the house alone for five minutes, then fifteen, and so forth until he is relaxed enough to be left alone for several hours at a time.

2. For your puppy, being home alone can be a good feeling. This can be achieved by linking a constructive relationship with that of you being abroad. Before leaving the house, give your dog a new treat. When you are alone, provide him with various toys to equate the toys with you going out and leaving him. Another solution is to supply him with his favorite cookie or a hollow bone full of tempting treats that will take the dog a while to consume. Another solution is to supply him with his favorite cookie or a hollow bone filled with tempting treats that would take the dog a while to complete. Both are two fun games that can rid him of the emotions of discomfort and apprehension that your dog will indulge in.

3. Even your dog has to be contained while you are not around. Make sure to build a good connection for space if you need to do this. Please let him feel like he is moving to a lovely spot. Please do not place your dog in a cage; otherwise, his feelings of isolation can intensify. Choose a safe space instead of where he feels comfortable, and make it a point to spend some time playing with him in that room while you are home, so he can equate the space with fun.

4. Do not do the activities like leaving the house is a big problem for your dog, and avoid feeling guilty. Do not talk

to your dog for a few minutes before leaving the house and then another ten minutes when returning home. This will eliminate the excitement of you going away and coming back.

5. Another way to alleviate your dog's sensation of anxiety is to give him adequate exercise, usually before you leave the house. Your dog would be comfortable and exhausted after having him out for a jog or a brisk stroll, ready for a long nap when you are gone.

Separation anxiety occurs when dogs are frightened and distressed at the absence of their owner. This kind of attachment problem can be mild or severe. When the dog is quiet, over-grooming, and panting, a soft case is shown, while a severe separation anxiety case may be quite a struggle for the trainer.

The dog poisons the house, barks or howls nonstop, and ruins the house's furniture and other items.

After being left alone for just ten to fifteen minutes,

the dog also continues to exhibit behaviors consistent with separation anxiety.

Dogs who are most at risk of experiencing separation anxiety are those who saved most of their lives from shelters, lived in the streets, or trapped inside a cage or kennel.

And because this behavior only happens while the dog is left alone, there is nothing you can do to deter it from ruining your home any time you leave the house or annoying the neighbors.

However, during your absence, you should teach
your dog not to be afraid or fear.

Here are five ways that can help.

1. Some dogs feel relaxed being confined to a small
   room in the backyard, such as a cage or a small
   gated section of the property, and others feel
   comfortable. When the dog starts to get upset, let it
   out and do not want and push it because it will only
   worsen.

2. In certain situations, it is enough to confine the dog
   to a small space where he has access to the outside
   world to help him more secure and alleviate fear
   over the separation. In front of a glass door or a
   transparent window, you can position his crate or
   crib.

3. Owing to loneliness, many dogs suffer from
   separation anxiety. Find work that can be handled
   by your puppy. Teach him how to play "Find it, "-a
   game that he should play. If you want to play the
   game, you have to hide his favorite bones or stuffed
   treats where he can reach them. Using three or five
   bones or treats to keep him occupied (depending on
   how long you will be gone from home).

4. Providing your dog with lots of treats is another form of battling boredom. Rotate the toys to keep him from getting bored of playing with them. The opportunity to make your dog use his innate canine instincts when keeping him busy for hours is playing, biting, catching, and searching for his toys or treats.

5. Leave the television on or play chilling music. Studies have shown that soft, classical music relaxes dogs. Choose something that you listen to when you are at home, so your pet does not relate the music to your absence.

Separation Anxiety – Understanding Separation Anxiety Disorders In Dogs

Your dog can suffer from separation anxiety; often, puppies and dogs share a concern.

In the absence of his trainer, separation anxiety is a panic condition displayed by a dog.

It is the anxiety of being left alone that results in unwanted harmful actions. Lately, you have found that he gets aggressive all over the property when he's left home except for a few hours.

You come home, and it looks like a storm struck the house-papers littered all over it, the garbage can was knocked down, and your clothes were chewed into shreds.

Your dog can suffer from separation anxiety; often, puppies and dogs share a concern.

In the absence of his trainer, separation anxiety is a panic condition displayed by a dog.

It is the anxiety of being left alone

that results in unwanted harmful actions.

Dogs are interactive.

It is usual for them as puppies to become dependent and attached to their mother and their littermates.

This form of attachment is passed when the puppy enters your life to you, his owner. Everytime the dog is left alone in the household, this attachment results in discomfort, which is the most common separation anxiety source.

How to recognize separation anxiety

If your dog exhibits the following signs: destructiveness; constant screaming, shouting, howling, moaning, house soiling, pacing, depression, self-mutilation, excessive salivation, hyperactivity, and scraping or chewing on walls, doors, windows, chairs, and other things, your dog suffers from separation anxiety.

Causes Of Separation Anxiety

In dogs, there are multiple sources of fear over the separation.

Many were created from encounters before the dog ever became part of the family, such as the previous owner's death or abandonment.

Six other causes of anxiety in dogs are listed below:

1) A stressful incident that occurred when you were out, such
2) as an accident, a thunderstorm, or an alarm device was going off.
3) A failure or the inclusion of a member of the family.
4) Premature separation from the littermates and their mum.
5) Getting a new puppy in the home and spending many hours and little time with the new pet.
6) A drastic alteration in timetable, lifestyle, or atmosphere.
7) Changes that come from aging develop in older dogs, both physiologically and psychologically.

Chapter nine: Training your dog to sleep

Bringing a new puppy home will be an excellent time for the whole family.

You and your children will have the ability to experience this new addition, show them new tricks, play with them, and give them infinite affection.

Until they take the plunge, many families talk of having a new puppy

for a long time, and they think that the entire thing will be fine.

Although it is a beautiful idea to get the puppy around, several individuals start regretting it after a few nights of hardly getting to sleep.

You probably feel tired and hopeless between watching the dog whining and standing up and taking them to the toilet many times.

The good news is that the tips and strategies you need to turn it all around are here. To help them get their puppies to sleep, we will take some time to look at the stuff you need to do and the three main methods that perform the best for most families.

You will be sure to find a sleep training plan for your puppy that will work like a charm and help you, your family, and the puppy gradually get some much-needed sleep through the night, from the light sleeper system to the alarm clock method to the heavy sleeper method.

If you've brought a new puppy and are able to actually get some sleep and feel more refreshed and pleased with getting a puppy at home, be sure to check out this guidebook to learn all the steps you need to follow to start your puppy's sleep training today!

The Benefits Of Sleep Training Your Puppy

Sleep training your puppy is so important to everyone in the whole family. It helps to stop the whining from your puppy and allow you, your family, and even the puppy to get on a good schedule together, including plenty of sleep. There are many benefits to everyone in the family, including the puppy, forgetting the puppy on a good sleep schedule.

Some of these benefits of sleep training your puppy include:

It helps you get more sleep: If you have spent a few nights listening to the puppy and having to take them outside a million times each night, you are probably feeling pretty exhausted at this point. While sleep training methods still take a few more days before you see them completed, they are the right steps that you need to take to get your nights back on some excellent sleeping finally.

Can avoid accidents at night: If your puppy is up and moving and active in the middle of the night most nights, it will not be long before they have an accident. The more that the puppy is up, the more likely that they will have this accident. With the right sleep training procedure, you not only help teach your puppy how to sleep through the night, but you also help to train them to go outside at certain times so you will deal with fewer accidents.

Let's the family sleep: Not only do you need to get some sleep, but so does the rest of your family. If everyone is up in the middle of the night because the puppy is barking and making too much noise, it can be hard on everyone. Even if you are the only one getting up in the middle of the night to take care of the puppy, it does not mean that others are not hearing the puppy whine and bark and moving around. And it will not take long before this starts to wear on everyone's nerves. Helping the puppy learn how to sleep train can make a difference in the quality of sleep that everyone in the family can get. Helps your puppy get their days and nights in order: Just like you and others in your family need to get enough sleep at night so that you are all energized and ready to tackle the day, so does your puppy. If they get things mixed up, they will miss out on a lot of fun during the day playing with other people, going on walks, and more. Helping them learn to sleep through the night with sleep training can get them on a good schedule and make life easier for them and you.

Allows the puppy to be comfortable in their new home: When the puppy has some order and knows how things should be done and where they should do them, they are more likely to feel comfortable. And sleep training will make this process easier.

Allows for different times for play and sleep: You need to make sure that your puppy knows that there are times for sleeping, times for eating, times for playing, and so on. Some puppies sleep so much during the day that they get things confused and will have almost unlimited energy in the middle of the night. Unless you want to be up with them all night and then head into work, it is best to start working on a sleep training program with them right away. When the puppy learns to sleep properly at night, they are more likely to remember that daytime is the best time to play.

When It Comes to sleep training, there are so many things to keep in mind. But remember the benefits, and how much extra sleep you will be able to get when it is all done will make the whole process worth it.To make sure that you can get your puppy to fall asleep and sleep well during the night, there are specific steps that you can take during the day. If your puppy spends all day sleeping, and they do not get enough chances to go outside and go potty, or even if they eat or drink when it is close to their bedtime, then you are in for a long night. With some good planning and some positive actions during the first few days with your puppy, it will not take too much before your puppy falls asleep and stays asleep through the night.

What to do first is to understand if the puppy is active and busy during the day. If they are an older puppy or an adult dog transitioning into your home, make sure to take them on long walks, as long as they do not seem overwhelmed or stressed by the surroundings. On the other hand, with a new puppy, you may not be able to take them out on walks yet because they are not adequately trained to walk with a leash, and they may not have their vaccinations to keep them healthy.

If This Is the case with your puppy, you will need to find ways to keep the puppy moving. You can play with the puppy, have some people over to meet the puppy, and give them lots of chew bones and toys to play with. If you are not at home and can't keep the puppy active during the day, see if some friends or neighbors can do this for you. A dog sitter can be friendly to make sure your puppy is as active as possible during the day.
NOW, some puppies are energetic and love to bounce around and play all day. Others may be a little more mellow and may need some convincing to stay active rather than falling asleep during the day. Sometimes it is as easy as changing the environment that is around the puppy. If they like to get cozy in the house and sleep, then take them out back to see the new sounds, smells, and sights.

OF COURSE, it is essential to remember that your puppy does need a lot of sleep, so some small naps are perfectly regular. As long as they are not napping all day and they get up and move around enough, it is acceptable for them to have those naps. However, about three to four hours before you want to go to bed, do not let the puppy sleep. If you let the puppy sleep too much right before bedtime, they will have a hard time sleeping when you want them to.

Another Thing that you should remember here is that what goes in needs to come out. If you are right about setting up a water and food schedule for the puppy during the day, it can help prevent surprises in the middle of the night. Most puppies are going to eat somewhere between three and four meals a day. You must make sure that this last meal is at least a few hours before they go to bed. This allows the puppy to have some time to empty themselves before it is time to go to bed; three hours before bedtime is best, but try not to let it get any closer than an hour or two. If you are concerned about this eating schedule, it is best to talk with your vet to see what they recommend.

You Will Find that the whole process of feeding the puppy is going to need some trial and error. Not all puppies are going to respond to the same type of feeding schedule. If you find that your puppy needs to eat right before bed or closer to bedtime than the three hours, try to make that meal smaller. This can help them to make it through the night.

If You Have a puppy who wakes up in the middle of the night fussing because they are hungry, then pushing the eating time back to three hours before bedtime may not be the best. You can also try to give your pet some small snacks, like dog biscuits, right before they fall asleep. This is an excellent way to settle their tummy, and even a little water is known to help. Just make sure that they are not eating or drinking a whole bowl right before bed, or you will be up during the night many times.

The area where you will put the puppy down to sleep needs to be calm and relaxing. It should not have all their toys around it, and you should not spend the daytime hours making it fun to use. If you put toys into the sleeping area, you will find that the puppy wants to be playful and active. And if you often play in the bedroom, how is the puppy supposed to learn the difference between playtime and bedtime. There should be separate areas for playtime and sleep time. It is fair to hang out or cuddle with the puppy in the sleeping area during the day, but no games, such as tug of war or wrestling with toys in that area, or you will have one confused puppy.

One Project that you should concentrate on during those first few weeks with the puppy during the day is to teach them the command you want to use when it is time to go potty. This will be useful because it helps you to get the puppy outside and to use the bathroom before bedtime. This will take a few weeks for the puppy to learn how to associate the word with the action, so be patient and keep trying. Once they have been trained with that word, make sure to use it before bedtime to help the puppy relieve themselves.

And Of Course, you need to spend some time acclimating your puppy to their pen or crate if this is where you want the puppy to sleep at night. They need to be comfortable with the crate or the pen; otherwise, they will get nervous and not easily fall asleep. With a new puppy, all these experiences are new to them so take it slowly, follow the lead for your puppy, and show them what you expect. But making sure that they have a comfortable place to fall asleep at night will make a big difference in whether they fall asleep, stay asleep, or whining and causing you to be up most of the night instead.

If You Do Not Have a good day with the puppy, it will be tough to get them to fall asleep for you when night time comes around. Think this, if you spend all day sleeping, how likely is it that you will spend the night sleeping as well? Just because you were busy and active at work all day does not mean that your puppy got all that activity while they were home alone. You must make sure that at night they are worn out, so they are more able to sleep.

You can opt for different solutions, and we spent some time talking about them already. You can take them on a walk when you first get home. This is good for both of you to do. If you have a puppy, make sure to leash them first, so they are more comfortable walking and only go the distance they are comfortable with. If this is pretty short, you could do a quick walk when you first get home and then a longer one before bed to wear them out. As they get older, you can make the hike longer and get in some exercise.

Playtime Is essential as well. If you have any children, include them in on this to have some fun. Have a variety of toys for the puppy to play with, both inside and outside, and just have some fun. You can play fetch, tug of war, or anything that gets the puppy up and moving. Just make sure that you simmer it down and relax a bit from the wild games right before bed, or the puppy will be too hyper to calm down and go to sleep.

Training the puppy can be a good idea during this time as well. This helps to get rid of some of the pent-up energy they have, but it can also help them work out their minds, making them sleepy. Start with some of the most simple commands, such as staying, sitting, rolling over, shaking, and then building up or practicing those as you are ready. Include everyone in the family to teach the puppy some new tricks, and the puppy learns that everyone can be in charge of the home.

Of Course, always remember not to feed the puppy too much and too close to the bed. The puppy does not want to be hungry, so if they fill up too much right before bed with food and snacks, it will only be a few hours before they are ready to get up and be let out again. Allow enough time before bed for the puppy to eat and then go to the bathroom a few hours later to relieve themselves so they will sleep better.

Finally, take some time to make their room or sleeping area as comfortable as possible. With a puppy you just brought home, you may want to let them sleep with you and then move them to another place or their crate later on. You can make a decision; just make sure that the puppy will be comfortable in their sleeping arrangements before it is time to go to bed.

This May Seem like a lot of work initially, but it is necessary to ensure that your puppy feels good and will get some good sleep at night. The more active you can keep your dogs, the more comfortable their bed, and the less they must go to the bathroom before bed, the better you will sleep that night.

Where should my puppy sleep?

The next issue to consider is where you would like to put the puppy to sleep. This location is going to depend on you and your family. Some families want to have the puppy right next to them so they can spend more time together. Others are not that fond of the idea of having a shedding or snoring beast in their bedrooms, so they will pick another location. You can choose among many options when it comes to select the sleeping place for your puppy, and you need to select the one you think works the best.

FIRST, you must decide where the puppy needs to sleep, right from the start. This might or not be the same area you want to use when you pick a spot for them permanently because sometimes it is best to keep the puppy near you when they first come home. Most dogs are considered pack animals, and they feel more comfortable when they can be near other people.

This Is true even you are dealing with a puppy or a grown dog. Some people choose to keep the puppy in the same room as well into adulthood just because it feels more comfortable for the dog and can make sleeping at night easier on everyone in the home.

You Can Always Move the puppy to another place in the home once they are older and more comfortable. Even when you do not plan to make this a permanent thing, having the puppy spend the first few nights with them can help them feel more secure and comfortable in this new environment and help them make it through the night faster.

If You Do Decide to have the puppy sleep in one place, and then you want to change that location later when the puppy gets older, that is fine. But you must remember that this is going to add some more steps to the process. You may find that you have to retrain the puppy again to get them used to a new sleeping location.

SOME PUPPIES DO this well, and it only takes a few nights or so to get them to switch over. Others may need to go through the process repeatedly to get comfortable with a new sleeping location. It is fair to go through this to get them in the right spot; it is just something that you need to keep in mind when choosing a place.

After You Have Had some time to train the puppy and show them how to sleep through the night, then you can make a personal decision about where they should sleep on a more permanent basis. You could choose to let the puppy continue sleeping with you as this is considered beneficial to them, but if another room in the home works better, this is fine as well. You can choose a place such as a laundry room, kitchen, or another chosen room. Some owners decide to let their dogs have free reign to sleep where they want at night, but you must make sure that you have broken them of destructive habits.

No Matter where you choose to have the puppy sleep when they are young, and first getting started, you must confine them somehow. Otherwise, you are going to find a mess, including chewed-up shoes, all over the home. Some of the places you can choose that will ensure that your puppy stays safe, comfy, and won't get into trouble include:

Inside their crate: if you are already working to crate train your puppy, it is just fine if you choose to have them sleep in this crate. Just make sure that this place is comfortable for them. Add in a few soft toys for company, some good bedding, and that the puppy has had some exposure to this crate before you try to make them sleep in there. You can also consider turning the box so that the puppy can see you while they are sleeping.

In pen: A wire exercise pen can be an excellent place to put the puppy to sleep if you use potty pads to teach them how to use the bathroom. You can pick out a pen for them to sleep in at night, as long as it is just large enough to fit the potty pads and the blanket for them to sleep on. This will help the puppy to find them sleeping and potty arrangements faster. If you use a pen, set it up in the area you want to use permanently to make the puppy more comfortable.

Dog bed: If you would like to start having your puppy sleep in a dog bed, you do not want to set it down and hope that it will all work out. Make sure that the mattress is somewhat confined so that they cannot wander off and make a mess. One good idea is to set up the dog bed between the wall and your bed. This allows for a small area where you can place the ground, and then you just have a little space to block off with a gate or some kind of barrier.

In your bed: Some people choose to have the puppy sleep in their bed, either temporarily when they get accustomed to the new environment or permanently. You must make sure that you can keep the puppy on the bed so they do not wander off while you are sleeping and cause a mess and so that they do not fall off the ground and get hurt. Most of the time, it is best for you just to save this until the dog is older and can handle staying asleep on the bed.

As You Can See, there are some different options that you can use when it comes to training your puppy and where you would like them to sleep. Sometimes, the method you use when you first bring the puppy home will be different from the options you resort to later on when the puppy is trained and a little bigger. You can choose the method that seems to work the best for you and your family and the puppy so that you can finally get some sleep at night.

Preparing Your Puppy For Bed

Now that you have been learning about getting your puppy prepared to go to bed at night and even thought of some places where you would like the puppy to sleep, it is time to prepare your puppy for the foundation of the best results. As It Gets close to bedtime, a little planning and preparation will make sure that you and your puppy will be able to get a good night's sleep. It is not going to work just to hope that the puppy will fall asleep just like you. You do need to put in a little bit of work to see it become a reality.

There is something essential that you need to consider before you get started with any of this. You need to set a bedtime that is reasonable for your puppy. You must also have reasonable expectations for how long the puppy will be able to sleep at night. So, just because you put the puppy down for bed at eight does not mean that they will be entirely asleep for the rest of the night. If they go to sleep, they will probably be up at two in the morning, ready to play. Many people have trouble keeping their puppies asleep during the night and do not understand that they are letting the puppy go to bed too early. If you go to bed at eleven at night but expect the puppy to go to sleep at night and still sleep until you get up, that is too long. Most puppies will not make it past six or seven hours, maybe eight as they get older, before they need to go to the bathroom. It is usually best to schedule the puppy to go to bed when you sleep to make life easier.

While you are getting ready for bed, set out some of the things you may need in the middle of the night. It is likely that when you have a new puppy, you will need to get up a few times to let them out. Rather than fumbling around in the dark when they are ready to go out, make sure that everything is set and that you have a nice clear path to walk through at night.

You can prepare some things to do this. For example, unless your backyard is covered completely and you live in an area that gets nice temperatures, you should make sure that you have a robe or something else to wear while you are in the backyard. You can also keep your shoes, glasses, treats, and other things right there if you need it. If you are going somewhere that does not have the best light, consider having a flashlight ready to see what the puppy is doing and make sure that they will not get lost while going potty. While you are doing it, make sure that the path that goes from your bed to wherever the puppy is located is as clear as possible. Tripping can be a hazard when you get up with the puppy in the middle of the night. You can even consider having a nightlight around to make it easier to see what is going on around you when you get up in the middle of the night.

Another thing to consider is having either a white noise machine or a loud fan ready to go wherever the puppy is going to be sleeping. This is a big help because the steady noise is soothing for most puppies and is good at masking some of the outside noises and may wake up the puppy. If you choose to use a fan for this, make sure that it is pointed away from the puppy, so they do not get cold.

You can also consider using a towel or a blanket. If you notice that the puppy seems a little fussy in their crate and they do not need to be let out to go potty, they may do better if you take the time to cover their crate. For some puppies, this is calming. Just make sure that you check the crate to see if there is enough airflow and that the temperatures will not get too hot inside the crate.

Some people have also tried another trick. For this, they will take a ricking close and a hot water bottle, wrap them in a towel, and put them in with the puppy to help make it easier to sleep at night. According to some dog owners, the point of doing this is to help the puppy remember the heartbeat and warmth of their mommy to get comfortable and go to sleep. The puppy will be reminded of their mother and the warmth and comfort they felt when they were with her, and for some puppies, this is the easiest way to get them to fall asleep.

Studies are still out on whether this one will work, but it certainly will not hurt anything to give it a try if you like the idea. You can even try using a plush puppy sleep toy that has a warmer or a heartbeat inside so that your puppy can enjoy a little bit of company while they are sleeping at night. And Of Course, the final thing that you must do before you put the puppy down after their beds are as comfortable as possible is to take them out one more time to go to the potty. Do this about ten to fifteen minutes before bed, and then again right before bed, so that the puppy has plenty of time to go and can get all those distractions out of the way. This helps empty the puppy and save you many hassles and possible accidents when you wake up in the morning. When you have a little dog to contend with, likely, you will still need to get up a few times at night to take them out, but it won't be long before you can stop doing this as well.

Setting things up so that the puppy can easily go to sleep can make such a difference in how much sleep you get. Ensure that the puppy does not nap too much, stay up long enough at night, have an empty bladder, and are as comfortable as possible.

Coming up with a plan

A t this point, it is time to make your plan for surviving the night with a new puppy. You can use three methods, but before we get into a discussion about each one, here are a few basics that will apply to all the overnight training methods, no matter which path you decide is the best for you.

First, you need to consider the situation and what your puppy is going through. You likely got the puppy right from their mother, and they are used to having that warmth and the warmth of their littermates around them. Even if you had a stray who you got from the pound or a shelter, you are still bringing them into a new environment that they may be a bit cautious about.

What this means is that the first step you should take for sleep training will include spending time soothing and comforting the new puppy to relax before learning that night is when they should sleep. You most likely will need to let them sleep next to you for company, even if you want to have them sleep in their room later on.

One Worry here is that you will spoil the puppy and never train them to sleep independently. The truth is, the puppy will have a better time sleeping on their own later on if they got to spend the beginning time with you compared to those who were left alone right from the beginning. Even if you spend just a few nights sleeping with the puppy, it still gives them some comfort and confidence in their new environment.

Once you notice that the puppy is sleeping pretty good and you would like to get them to start sleeping on their own, it is important to do so in small steps. For example, if the puppy is sleeping in your bed and wants to get them to start sleeping in their crate in another room, the first step would be to get the dog used to be in the crate during the day. Then you can move the crate to the side of the bed and have them stay there at night.

After the puppy has been able to do that, then you can move the puppy and the crate to their permanent sleeping room on a night when they are really tired. This is a day that you should get them extra tired to not nap during the day. This makes it more likely that the puppy will go straight into the crate and fall asleep without any issues because they are too tired to fight.

With a small puppy, you will need to get up and take them to the potty at least once or twice a night. When you do this, it is best to get them while they are still asleep or when they are reasonably calm if you can. It makes it much smoother to let the puppy fall asleep until they are finished. If you wait too long and the puppy is screaming and freaking out, you will find that they are now too wound up to go to sleep, and it could lead to a very long night for you.

From here, it is time to decide which method you would like to choose so that you can get your puppy to sleep well through the night. All puppies and their owners will be different, so you may find that you like one method better than the other, or you may need to do some trial and error. No one method is better than the other, so go ahead and try them out and see what works the best for you!

The Best Sleep Training Techniques For Your Puppy

The Alarm Clock Method is considered one of the best methods to use because it is so simple, and you will not have to remember a ton of steps to get it done. It is easy, but maybe not fun, but it is considered effective and simple to follow.

When you use this method, you will be able to take control over the overnight schedule for your puppy by setting the alarm clock to help wake you up each night. It does not matter if the puppy wakes up or not. The point here is to beat the puppy to the goal. If your puppy wakes up before you, it is uncomfortable, and they will probably get hyper and freak out, making it hard for you to get them back to sleep in the end.

By setting the alarm and waking up before the puppy does to take them out, you can save many hassles. First, the puppy will still be sleepy and easier to get to bed in the middle of the night when they are done. Second, the puppy never gets in the habit of crying and barking to wake you up.

When bringing the puppy home for the first time, you will likely need to have the alarm go off for you a few times each night. You will need to do this every two hours for a puppy who is between seven to nine weeks old. Once the puppy is between nine weeks to fourteen weeks, you can do it every three hours. And puppies that are over fourteen weeks will go about every four hours.

Of course, these are pretty general guidelines for a brand-new puppy: some need to go more often, and some need to go less. Take the time to learn the schedule of your puppy so you can set the alarm at the right time and take them out before they wake up and get too hyper. If you have already had the puppy for a few weeks, then it is likely that you already know how long the puppy can hold it, so base the schedule you use on that.

So, if the puppy has gotten into the habit of waking you up with barks and crying every four hours, then you should set the alarm for every three or three and a half hours. The exact time is not important, as long as you make it your goal to catch the puppy when they are likely to need to go, but before they get to a critical point of howling and barking.

Once The Puppy is on a good schedule of waking up at intervals throughout the night, you are going to work on pushing it to get the puppy to sleep longer. In the beginning, you may be tired of waking up so often, but this is the part of the program when the work will pay off. Since you are the one who is in control of the schedule at night, you can adjust the wake-up times and then work through until you get the puppy to start sleeping through the whole night.

For Most Puppies, once you can wake up the puppy and get them to go potty at night on a schedule, without accidents, to howl or barking, for three nights, then it is time to move on. However, when you go with this process for very young puppies, it is better to wait for about five nights in a row before moving on.

When You Are ready to extend this, you will want to extend how long you wait before waking them up by about thirty minutes each time. So, if you were successful at waking the puppy up at 1:00, 3:00, and 5:00, you will now go through and wake them up at 1:30, 4, and 6:30. Once you have another three to five nights of this, you can increase it all by another thirty minutes again.

You will keep moving these potty trips ahead until the last trip that you have started to coincide with the time you want to get up in the morning. At this point, you should not be down to two potty trips instead of having to do three. And over time, you will go down to one until you are finally down to none.
One downside that you should know about this method is that you may get up more often at night and take the puppy to the bathroom more times than they need. This is especially true if you

start this from the moment you bring the puppy home and have no idea what their schedule is about. There is nothing wrong with the puppy being let out more often than they need to go in the long-term. You will miss out on more sleep in the short-term, but this process does not last long, and you will make it up.

The Light Sleeper Method

If you do not appreciate the idea of setting your alarm clock to wake up all those times in the middle of the night, then it may be time to try a different method. Some people do not like the other method because they see that waking up by an alarm many times at night is stressful or wasting their time by taking the puppy outside too often. The following method will work great if you are a pretty light sleeper, and you are going to let the puppy sleep near you. When it comes to the light sleeper method, you will let the puppy tell you when they are ready to go potty so that you can take them to the right potty spots when needed. When you start to hear the puppy moving around in their pen or their crate at night, or if you hear a bit of light painting or whimpering, then you must get out of their bad as soon as possible and take the puppy out.

To see success with this method, you need to be a light sleeper to notice when the puppy starts to move around. If you sleep too deeply, then the puppy will start to wail and shriek to be taken out, and then they will be stressed and wide awake when they are done. This will also teach the puppy that it is fine to wake you up with hysterics, which will get old pretty fast when the puppy decides they want attention later on.

The nice part about using this method is that if you use it the right way, you can save some hassle and will only take the puppy out when they really need to go. Get one of those puppies who can go for longer periods for their age without needing to be let out. This method will allow you to get more sleep because you will not need to make unnecessary trips outside, resulting in a puppy that sleeps through the night very quickly.

However, there are a few downsides when this method. If the puppy does not move around a lot when they wake up or find that you are not really as the light of a sleeper as you thought, you could end up with a puppy who will work themselves up to crying before you even notice something is wrong.

It is still a good idea to wake up and take the puppy out if this happens, but it may be time to rethink whether this is a good method if this happens more than once or twice. Another issue is that you may have a puppy who doesn't want to wake you or make a lot of noise and who will instead just have an accident right where they are without you noticing. If this does happen to you, then this isn't the right method for your little puppy, and it may be best to work with the alarm clock method to help get on a schedule.

The Heavy Sleeper Method

The third method that you can choose is the heavy sleeper method. This is usually not seen as the most effective method to sleep train your puppy, but it can work for some people. This is sometimes the only thing that will work if you have a puppy that is really fussy, loud, or resistant to other approaches. This is often a method that you will resort to when others do not work.

For this method, spend the first three to five nights sleeping with the puppy so that they can get used to being in your home and their new surroundings. When that is done, this method will require that the puppy will sleep in another room. Pick out a room that is at least far enough away from you that you will not be able to hear them crying. You can place the puppy into a pen, a crate, or a small puppy-proofed room, such as a laundry room, depending on what housebreaking program you choose.

No matter what room you choose to go with, it is important to make sure that the puppy is getting a comfortable place to stick with. You should also make sure that the puppy is also getting enough chances to go to the potty during the night. However, if you hear the puppy scream bloody murder because they are not that fond of sleeping at night, you will just leave them in the other room so that they can cry it out.

This method requires the puppy to be in another room so that you can ignore the crying and get some sleep. If they need to, encourage them to go to the toilet, but some puppies just like to be noisy and struggle to go to sleep. This could easily keep you up at night and can make it difficult for everyone. If you have a light sleep, you can turn on a sound machine, a loud fan, a radio, or even wear some earplugs. If you do this, set an alarm clock that is loud enough that you can hear it, and then use the alarm clock method so that the puppy can go out to the potty at the right times.

After you take the puppy out for their bathroom break based on the alarm clock method, put the puppy right back to the crate or pen or room, and then go back to bed. You will be shocked by how easily the puppy will get through this screaming period, especially when they learn that it is not actually done by their noise. Know that after a matter of days, some puppies may get through this while others can take a couple of weeks.

The good news that the puppy will get over this, even if it seems like it takes some time. It will just take each puppy a different amount of time. Once the puppy has resigned themselves to the fate and starts to sleep at night, you get the choice to have them stay sleeping in that same area, or you can move them closer to you or a new location if you choose. You just need to get through the whining part, and separating the puppy from you can make that process a bit easier.

There are some downsides to this. The big downside to this is that if the puppy does end up waking up at night and makes noise because they need to go potty, even if it is not on your schedule, it is likely that you are not going to be able to hear them. This means that you will run into a big risk of the puppy having an accident because they cannot go out when they really need to go.

You might run into some issues with your neighbors that may not be happy with the wailing that the puppy has. If you are not careful with this, you could end up with a neighbor who is upset and banging on your door in the middle of the night. Before you go with this method, consider who else may be bothered by the crying puppy if you put them in another room and ignore them. If the puppy only whines for a few nights, you are probably fine. But if they are really resistant and cry for a few weeks, the neighbors are not likely to be that happy.

These three methods are meant to help you get your puppy to start sleeping through the night. Each of them will take some time to accomplish and will not get the puppy to start sleeping through the night in one night. But with some work and some dedication, and by following the suggestions in each of the steps, you will be able to get that puppy to sleep through the night in less time than you would imagine.

What To Do If It's Not Working?

I f you have turned straight to this page because you are already in the middle of the mess with a puppy who won't sleep, you may be in panic mode. You will not be able to go through and try any of the tips until you can read this book, and that will not happen until tomorrow. So, you may be wondering what steps you can take to help make things easier today.

The first thing to consider is going to pick up the puppy and give them a little bit of attention. Depending on how much time you have spent with them so far today and how active they have been, you may also need to go and get them a bit of exercise. You may think that this is a bad thing, and you may be teaching the puppy that they will get their way if they make a lot of noise. However, you need to do it anyway.

For Tonight, until you can get some time to read the book and implement the steps that we talked about above, you will just give in so that you and the puppy can get a little bit of relief for the night. When you wake up in the morning, it is time to start it all fresh and use the tips that are in this guidebook. Since you have not even started on the training program at all, getting the puppy this once when they are crying will not undermine anything.

Plenty of people do this for weeks before they start on a training program, so doing it once is not that big of a deal. Once you pick one of the above sleep training programs, do not do this anymore. But for tonight, so that the two of you can get some sleep, it is just fine to give the puppy some love and attention.

Now, if your puppy did not get a lot of napping in during the day and they were pretty active, at this point, they are probably tired but have just become too stressed out and scared about the new sleeping environment. You may find that the puppy will easily settle down once you let them spend some time near you. If you want him to sleep on the floor next to the pen or crate to get them used to this new place, you can pick. You can also tether them in the bed so they do not move and fall off. Sometimes moving the crate by the bed or elevating it on a chair so that the puppy can see you will help. Choose the technique that suits you better when it comes to the puppy.

If you do this and you are a bit worried about how the puppy may wake up everyone in the family if you place them in your room, or you do not like the idea of letting a dog be in your room, you can just set up camp in the living room. For this, you would simply get comfortable on the floor or the couch and let the puppy sleep next to you. You can also let the puppy be in the crate, and you can try sticking your fingers in to let the puppy know you are there.

The point here is that the puppy will often calm down when they know that someone is there and that they are not alone in a new environment. You may have to be uncomfortable for a night or sleep somewhere new in the home, but it is often enough to get the puppy to fall asleep, and then everyone in the home can get some peace.

On the o, if your puppy is still awake late at night and they did get plenty of naps in during the day, they may not want to settle down even after spending some time near you. This is most likely because the puppy has plenty of energy to use, and they want to go and burn it off. Even if you are overly exhausted at this point, the best thing to do is to help them get that energy to go away. You can have some playtime or take them on a walk to not have the puppy barking and waking up everyone.

No one wants to go on a walk or play with a puppy when it is time to go to bed, but this is the best option if you have a puppy who slept too much during the day and has a lot of leftover energy to get rid of. If you do not have the time to wear out the dog, everyone else will get up and screw around all night long. It might be three in the morning, but as soon as you take some of the steps we discussed earlier, you will not have to have this busy time too early anymore. Once you have been able to get the puppy back to sleep and settle down, you can start to follow the instructions for puppy sleep training to get through the rest of the night.

Now, if your puppy went through a busy day and did not have many naps, and they are already sleeping right by you, but you still notice that they are freaking out, it may be a moment to change up the arrangements that you picked for sleeping. If the puppy is in a carte or a pen, they may not be comfortable in that yet and need to be tethered to a bed. Or, if you have already let them sleep by you for a few nights to help them adjust, you may want to consider trying the heavy sleeper training method so that they learn how to get used to their environment without disturbing your sleep.

If the puppy is brand new to your home, or they are showing signs that they are extremely stressed, then do not use the heavy sleeper method. If you notice shaking, trying to escape from a pen or crate in a manner that will hurt them, or lots of drooling, then you do not want to use that method. Instead, let the puppy stick next to you so that they do not get stressed out, and then consider using a dog trainer in the next few days. You will find that severe anxiety issues like this are hard to solve all on your own without experience, so if your puppy shows these signs, it may be time to bring in the professionals.

Also, if your puppy has been sleeping well, and then they wake up suddenly with cries, this is considered normal. You should just need to take them out to go to the bathroom and put them right back to bed. You only need to go with the instructions that we talked about above if your puppy has already gone to the bathroom and is still freaking out or if you just can't calm them down. You can always give them comfort for now and do whatever it takes to get some sleep, and then skip on to reading the tips in this book and following them later.

And remember, while you are doing all of this, make sure that the puppy is not crying because they are hurt or sick. Sometimes, the crying is because they are scared of getting your attention, which is normal. But if you see signs that your puppy is not feeling good or is in pain and seems to be crying because of this, it is important to get them to a vet.

The desperate measures

Now, if you have gone through all of the methods that are in this book and you are not getting good results after some reasonable time, you may be at a loss for what you should do next. This rarely happens, but with some puppies, it does. If this is the circumstance, it may be time to take it to the next level.

You may decide to consider working with a professional dog trainer to help you out at this POINT. Some will be willing to take the puppy home and do some of the initial steps that are needed for sleep training. This is only recommended if the trainer is going to have the puppy stay at their home rather than in a boarding kennel. You should also check with the trainer to make sure that they have experience doing this and have a training philosophy that matches your own. If you are interested in this, then talk to your vet or a friend to get some recommendations. If you are lucky to find someone who works for this, you could even have them do the first few nights of sleep training, or you can try a friend or family member to help. You may know someone who is able and willing to do the work and can make it a bit easier for you. Either way, it can take some of the pressure from you and make sleep training your puppy so much easier on the whole family.

Now, you may be worried about sending your puppy off for a few nights for training. This can be hard to send away the puppy, and you may feel that you are giving up the responsibility you should handle. However, in the real world, you sometimes need help and can't do it all on your own. Instead of having a few bad days and nights and then returning the puppy, getting some help at the beginning can make it easier and can make you and the puppy so much happier. The positive side is that it is rare to find an adult dog that doesn't know how to sleep through the night. So even though you have a sort of rocky start with the puppy and sleep training takes longer than you think it does, the good news is that the puppy will learn how to sleep through the night finally!

Chapter ten: Leash training

When walking down the street with its owner, pulling at the leash as it excitedly greets anyone who walks by? These little puppies put so much hat could be more adorable than a little 10-week-old German Retriever effort in seeing what happens around them, and they are always happy when we give a pat on their tiny head. This is all sweet, that is before the dog hits a bodyweight of 50 to 60 pounds and practically drags his trainer on the leash back across the street.

Now the once happy smiling woman grits her teeth and tries whatever she can to prevent the puppy from dragging her down the pavement.

If strangers pass by, the owner must hold the dog back from running and jumping all over these poor people. These sorts of dogs that do not have leash control inevitably waste all their time in the backyard without ever being exercised.

A dog's owner should start leash training from the very beginning. Many dog owners who buy a new puppy completely underestimate how necessary it is to spend time in leash training as early as possible, mostly because they have a pup that grows 6 to 10 times the puppy's size.

They do not know that the day their new dog comes home, training continues.

Any activities of a puppy will become a professional subconscious practice.

In time, even though it might be a wrong move that you disapprove of the dog would not think twice about what it is doing.

What do you foresee, in all honesty to the dog,

if you disregard sound parenting standards early in his life?

What alternative is there for a dog?

Having a proper leash is extremely important.

It can make or break dog training, whether you have the right kind of tools.

You can either make the training experience fun and productive, or a total waste of time, using the right resources.

What is the best leash for training?

Luckily, When it comes to leash systems, most of them can't go wrong.

However, for training purposes, there is one type of leash that is not recommended: the retractable type.

It is possible to find retractable leashes in every size and shape, extending at different lengths. This leash systems are essentially a plastic case that slips into your palm, which has a remote lever that releases the leash to stretch up to a certain length and can then be locked at the particular distance you choose.

Yes, these types of leashes can benefit many situations, but you need to have a leash that can constantly tension the dog's neck for training a new puppy or even an adult dog.

You also need to maintain a very short distance between you and your buddy, but this is very hard to do when using a retractable leash. With too much distance, your dog will have no concept that you are even walking with him.

Lastly, you must have consistent leash pressure and release moments for the dog to understand the commands you teach him, such as heeling. With a retractable leash, it can extend at different distances and be locked inconsistently. Your puppy may become frustrated as it perceives unfair and irregular corrections each time you vary the length and lock it in place.

Potential owners of dogs enormously overlook leash teaching.

It's pretty easy to get your puppy or adult dog used to be on a leash, and it only takes a little time.

Trust me, shortly, this small investment of adequately teaching your dog to walk respectfully on his leash would pay high returns, especially if your puppy grows up weighing 50 pounds or more. Down below, there are some of the most common questions about leash training. Know, when it comes to dog training, there is no right way to do it; whether it includes leash training or another tutorial, it's cool to throw in your training strategies as long as you keep it 100% optimistic. Negative training for dogs is not recommended and is too discouraged.

Common questions about leash training:

1. How much space should I give to the leash to extend when I walk my dog? Most trainers think that your puppy or adult dog does not need more than 6 feet of distance to keep when you are walking. This is a lot of space for the owner to keep control of the situation, and at the same time, you can give your dog time to sniff out areas while walking.

2. What kind of substance should be made of my dog's leash? You will find that most leashes for sale are made of nylon if you step into any pet-specific store. Nylon is very easy to wash and comes in all manner of fantastic shades. However, these leashes will burn your hand if the dog pulls suddenly and the cord passes between your fingers.

Using a leather leash is my suggestion. The right size and material is a 6-foot leash made out of leather.

It will last a long time, and if it is pulled, you will not feel some sort of burning feeling. The grip is firm, and it improves power.

What about using leashes for a chain?

Chain leashes are virtually indestructible and can last a very long time, but if the dog yanks hard and your hold breaks, a chain leash will damage your hands, much like nylon material.

Probably, the damage may be a lot more severe than a nylon burn.

How wide should the leash be? This answer is straightforward. A leash is suitable and is about ½ inches to ¾ inches. Try avoiding cumbersome, rigid leashes.

Do You Have The Right Mindset?

Training the dog's leash is much more than merely taking a few steps and directions.

It's the owner's right mentality that is the single most critical factor.

Progress or loss, pleasure, or rage depends on how you treat your puppy's walking sessions.

Launch your leash training off, so to say, on the right paw.

Let it first adapt to a buckle collar's sound if you have an odd puppy with a leash and collar.

Once the collar is comfortable to wear, clip on a short light line and watch as it drags it along.

A few days a day, keep the line on for 10-minute sessions until your dog no longer pays attention to it.

Again, let it have time to adjust to the feel of this new gadget before snapping on a leash with an older puppy or adult dog you've designed for a headcollar or prong collar.

Do not leave specialist collars on an unsupervised puppy.

Since all prongs and head collars tighten under pressure, a dog may suffer serious injury if the collar catches an obstacle.

At these get-comfortable sessions, pay particular attention to your dog. As teaching leash etiquette requires total discipline, you must approach training with the correct mindset.

Whether you plan on it or not, any walk becomes a training session.

When we walk after work, there is no such thing as "We train when we walk after work, but all the other walks are just walking."

As we are nervous, rushed, and sometimes doing something other than paying attention to our dog as it walks, this is a challenging idea for individuals. There should be no hurried walks and no breaks to talk with neighbors as your dog is studying, no use of time to make a call on your mobile phone, etc.

If you continuously neglect it, you can't trust your dog to become aware of you on a stroll.

Likewise, recognize that your dog doesn't pull on the leash to aggravate, annoy, punish or get back at you – it's merely a matter of cause and effect. The dog is thinking: I pull, you follow, and therefore, I get to where I want to go. You must reshape this thought process. Put emotions aside, view your lessons as an opportunity to forge a new relationship, and decide that from this day forward, you and your dog will learn how to enjoy your walking time together!

Leash Training 101: Start With The Correct Collar

One of the most efficient leash training methods that have been created today is that it encourages the dog to develop its owner's awareness. First, a stable, smooth, or rolled buckle collar made of leather or nylon should be used. Although familiar with obedience trainers, slip collars are not generally good options for teaching leash etiquette - which tightens and release in reaction to stress.

On the lead, most dogs are too excitable and sometimes tug carelessly against this form of harness, damaging the trachea sometimes.

This collar is better left to those seasoned in its use, though acceptable in the right hands.

The "headcollar" is the most potent teaching technique for the defined dog that already has a pulling habit.

This comparatively new invention loops through the collar and muzzle of the dog's top.

On either side of the head and one below the muzzle, the loops are connected by an extra strap.

The leash binds to the halter on the collar. The theory is based on the fundamental physical rule that the rest of the animal must obey where the head goes. Whenever friction is applied, the headcollar pushes the dog against the walker.

It tightens around the muzzle of the head and back, simultaneously allowing the dog to step in the direction of its owner to relieve the pain.

Initial hands-on training by a teacher familiar with its application, ideally developed to provide a soft alternative to most collars, is also a smart choice to get the best fit and more successful process. A prong, or pinch collar, may fit well for the standard size breed that

is about six months or older, and for the adult dog that naturally pulls.

This metal collar has wide prongs that turn inward around the dog's neck, producing what could be described as a blunted, teeth-like effect, made to constrict in response to applied stress, then expand instantly again when tautness is removed. Right fit and scale are significant, as with the headcollar, and are

best judged by a trainer well qualified in the proper use of prong-collar.

One who is too close always pinches the dog, which is detrimental to the dog's training and unfair. One that is too loose loses its efficiency. A well-fitted prong collar, just behind the head, should sit high on the dog's neck.

When pressure is not applied, you should be able to slide your fingertips beneath the neck, but it should not be kept so loose that it slides down across the trachea.

Despite its somewhat formidable look, the proper use of a prong collar encourages the dog to pause and consider its owner.

When friction is applied, the prongs just bite, such as when the dog pushes.

The pinch is directly related to the amount of pressure being applied.

The more friction is exerted, the more complicated the pinch will be. For leash training, prong collars perform best because the dog determines how much weight it places on its collar and monitors the amount of pinch it gets.

By retaining slack in the lead, helps the animal to escape the squeeze.

The Golden Rule

The majority of dog owners only discuss the leash training issue until it becomes an issue.

In the beginning, they initially think it's cute" while walking their dog that a puppy pulls away from the whole trip to the park because, they think, the dog "just can't wait to play with its ball." But after this pulling habit is ingrained, it takes time to retrain.

No matter what tools and training system you use when practicing leash etiquette, experts will advise you to abide by one cardinal rule: any dragging by the dog means all forward motion stops. You stop any time your puppy or dog places strain on the leash!

Oh, but instead of standing there and making this a war of wills, we adults outsmart our wise dogs and persuade them that it works in their favor to put slack on the lead.

Training would also provide treats, praise, and other beneficial payoffs.

Add A Clicker To The Mix

Enable your dog to understand that sticking next to you is a smart idea, that good stuff happens when you are nearby.

We recommend using a clicker, a lightweight, portable gadget that produces a "click" sound when pressed to accomplish this purpose. The click marks the desired action the second it happens and is followed by a treat automatically.

A clicker is an excellent way to break through the congestion of the world that is part of most leash walks, making the dog focused on you and what it does to get "paid."

When you become more attractive to your dog than anything

else the clicker helps teach your dog to ignore enticing obstacles.

Not unexpectedly, the best to train is a young dog who has never had a chance to develop the habit of pulling. Gather the teaching supplies first and snap the leash on the buckle necklace.

Start walking and speaking in a cheerful, polite voice to the puppy.

When he turns to look at you and goes slack with the leash, Click! This contact shows the dog that, yes, you are an essential part of walking. Note Repeated clicks and rewards while walking will help show your dog that within a one-foot circle of you, the big payoff usually occurs.

In the expectation of another reward, most pups will start to hang around.

Use food

While clicker training produces leash training outcomes, not everybody is happy with it.

Personally, when exercising my puppies, I do not use a clicker.

I would instead leave the benefits combined.

When you get the result you expect, a rub, compliment, toy, or food can be mixed up as prizes.

Food is excellent for luring a dog into behavior, but humans have a hard time getting rid of the treats once they have the concept.

Be unpredictable in your rewards; make a game of it.

Still stress upon the dog that when the leash is slack, the good stuff comes.

Learn how to use your facial gestures and voice so that your dog needs to be by you. There are instruments of preparation that you never leave at home. Train numerous pitches and sounds to see which can draw the attention of your puppy.

Many trainers have reservations over the use of treats, but the value of improving the standards must be recognized.

Before praising it, this involves telling the dog to do more.

As long as you continue to click and treat, your dog can learn to walk wonderfully by your side, so what happens when your pocket is empty? On each walk, attempt to make him do a little better, go a little faster between rewards, or ignore more significant distractions.

Your adult dog would require the same factors as a puppy during leash training, despite its age.

Help the dog appreciate that you have avoided using your voice to attract his attention as the rope goes taut.

If he is too busy barking or dragging things forward, he finds it incredibly tempting to use treats or a toy to divert him from his task. Before reaching the identified trouble spot, get these unique treats available to work to retain the interest of your dog. This will make the dog learn to disregard the noisy barking dog or the enticing nest of squirrels.

We just want immediate results, understandably, but dog training never works that way. It might take weeks or months to reassure the dog that pulling is not enough anymore. It will discourage owners to believe that they are doing something wrong or that their dog is helpless.. So in the end, even though the results are late to come, bear in mind that even two moves are advanced without pulling, and you have to praise, praise, and praise some more! Three steps will arrive soon, then four steps, and so on.

Overnight, in seven days or even a month, the transition is not going to be happy-it will take patience, justice, and continuity, meaning work nearly every day, even for months. Overall, gaining years of gains is a comparatively small cost. A deceptively tricky part of teaching is leash training. Dogs are learning to tug much faster than they are learning not to. The findings are worth it for those who devote the time and resources required to train leash etiquette.

Loose Leash Training

If the adults of your pup's breed are big and bulky, you'd better repair their pulling habit early.

Even if the breed is thin, painful pressure is concentrated on the dog's throat by habitual pulling against the neck.

This causes gasping and wheezing, and the airway of a dog can also fail and inflict irreversible injury.

The good news is it's not impossible to train your dog to walk nicely on a loose leash if you know a few tricks.

Old-style loose-leash walking training was focused on jerking the the collar of the dog with different degrees of intensity.

Although it will damage and harm your shoulders, knees, ears, or back by yanking a dog around your neck. Luckily, you can teach polite leash manners without having to jerk the leash. Several gentle, positive techniques for teaching loose-leash walking have been proven to work when consistently applied.

Starting with the right... Paw!

Believe it or not, most dogs tug the leash when they are taught by their trainers unintentionally.

Often individuals keeping the leash short and tight while attempting to restrain their dogs.

They train the dog to pull without understanding it by accustoming him to intense discomfort on the collar. Instead of discouraging dragging, the taut lead makes tightness the requirement on how a leash works.

Holding a tight leash, however, would not teach a dog to walk on a relaxed leash.

Guide your behavior toward healthy habits instead of making your pup develop bad habits.

Important Tip: About Leashes & Long Lines

For loose-leash walking exercise, many types of leashes can be used:

- 6-foot leash: This can be used either shortened or full-length and is long enough to tie to your belt for hands-free walking.
- 4-foot leash: This is similar to the 6-foot leash but less versatile
- 10 to the 30-foot long line: without pulling on some length of the leash, your dog will learn to walk. The long line enables regular supervision while enabling the dog space to explore.
- Retractable lead: These are handy, but the pulling dog controls them.
- Retractable contribute immediately to pulling on the leash to improve (reward). It undermines what you are trying to teach.

You are training your dog efficiently.

You can go for a fun stroll around the block when you place a leash on your dog, or is it more of a drag?

Walks do not have to become your puppy's tug-of-war.

Using these expert methods to train your little friend's loose-leash abilities

For the average dog owner to master, loose-leash walking is so complicated that they do not grasp the total importance of 100 percent accuracy.

It is easy to miss when you are occupied or frustrated and just let the dog pull away.

These intermittent lapses, while they perpetuate pulling, trigger training setbacks. If the dog learns that some of the time pulling works, it will keep checking to see if it works each time.

As soon as you click the leash on, dogs who have a developed pulling pattern frequently begin lunging ahead.

Retraining committed pullers who can not take more than one move without lunging will need super-human patience and pre-planning for any trip. For the owners who do not have a backyard who have to walk a dog many times a day is extremely challenging.

The trainer should use two distinct equipment sets for dogs like this: teaching friendly walking and handling the dog when you are too rushed or lazy to exercise.

Using a flat riding buckle collar and a no-pull belt or head halter for free walking if you have no time to practice.

The dog is permitted to walk the same way it is always walked while the free-walking equipment is used, so you must be 100 percent compliant in not allowing pulling when using the exercise equipment.

The dog must not get 1 inch closer to something it pulls against, either. When the dog gets better on the flat collar, there will soon be no use for the free-walking devices.

The most straightforward technique ever made.

One of the most common constructive strategies for teaching respectful leash walking is this. For puppies only learning to walk on-leash, it is particularly lovely. It is straightforward, but you need to be consistent. It is called the Stop-n-Go method, or the Tree Method, and it functions like this:

You have to pause and stand still if the dog places strain on the lead. You walk again as it finishes dragging. It is that! Simple, aren't they?

When you walk out again, the dog is thanked for walking on a loose leash. This approach trains the dog that pulling on the lead does not work. When the dog wants to hasten you by dragging, it takes longer to get there.

Setting a goal

On any walking route, some places are especially attractive to dogs. When dogs are near their favorite places, their excitement rises, and they will pull their owner. These areas can be used both as walking targets and as training incentives.

Start towards the desired target, such as a bush or clump of grass that all the dogs in the neighborhood leave "pee-mail." Stop walking just immediately your dog starts pulling you.

Stop for one second, so the dog is absolutely stopped, too, then turn around and walk the dog five paces farther from the target neutrally (non-grouchily). Mind the spot because for this training the session that will be your starting line.

Stand there for a second, then begin again to walk towards the target and repeat the lesson.

The moment you notice the tightness of the leash, stop walking, hesitate for a second, and then return to the starting line.

Your dog will find out how this game works a couple of days after it happens and will be able to take a few steps closer to the target each time.

Encourage your dog to sniff around and give it a few minutes to enjoy the spot until you hit the goal.

Be Unpredictable

The Stop-N-Go method (or Tree Method) often does not necessarily work at first on any dog, so your pup might not be paying attention. Personally, something occurred to me for my third puppy. I tried the Stop-N-Go strategy in the first place.

While when they were puppies, I found this approach works well for my other two dogs, it did not influence my more significant, more energetic Retriever. I argued that if I expected my dog to pay attention to what I was

trying to teach it, I was searching for a workable approach so that he could act interestingly.

This was when, so to say, I came up with the mad walk.

On an open space, this is better done, not on a short sidewalk.

It is a wild walk that is unpredictable.

I would go one step straight forward, one step 45 degrees to the left, one

step back, two steps straight forward, one step to the right, and so on.

I have varied the duration of my steps and the period at the same time.

I gradually raise the steps straight ahead until the dog is so confused that it begins paying constant attention.

The side and backward moves are finally discarded. The mad walk for your dog will take several weeks of training to realize that pulling does not get it where it wants to go.

Your puppy will sometimes get excited at times and resume pulling despite learning not to pull.

At all moments, use the mad walk to remind your dog that instead of dragging, it has to pay attention to you. Your dog must learn to walk with you while on-leash, not against you. The dog has to stay tuned to your vocal and hand gestures

and pace itself to your rhythm to keep the leash loose.

Michelle Kirk uses a training clicker (a tiny plastic gadget that produces a clicking sound as you press a button), a local pet sitter in Pacific Beach, San Diego, California, to teach dogs to walk on a loose leash.

Without any distractions, start in a peaceful place.

Start walking, then stop as the dog approaches the end of the rope before it tries to tug. Pause, wait for the moment when the dog turns its attention back to you.

Click at the first indication that the dog is moving its head in your direction, "At the first sign of the dog turning its head in your direction, click,"

Tip: A Quick Note About Collar Choices

Without making a few collar tips, a lecture on leash walking will not be complete.

Two primary forms of collar-those constrict as the leash is pulled and those that do not.

Obviously, for loose-leash training (or any training for that matter), the preferred collar we use is the non-constricting kind, only because it causes less pain and no unnecessary harm to the dog. They are made of leather or silk and are fastened with either a buckle or quick-release snap around the dog's collar.

The last tip to assist you with your dog's loose-leash exercise is to help your dog walk in a particular location.

Dawn Jecs, the dog trainer and owner of Puyallup, Washington's Chose To Heel, encourages dogs to walk around the handler in a particular position.

The leash is loose when they are in that position. She then teaches the dog to go to a place ahead of her left

foot, about 18 inches back and 18 inches ahead, before Dawn begins practicing leash walking.

This is close enough to hand a treat award to the dog or snap the leash on or off, but it's not underfoot far enough out.

Dawn celebrates it and gives it a reward when the dog goes to the spot, so the exercise stops. Without going on, Dawn repeats this before the dog goes quickly to the awarded spot.

With the same signal she used for driving, she teaches: "Let's go It automatically shifts into place as the dog hears the cue.

Then Dawn begins practicing with the leash.

It must be practice and effective with the leash loose for a dog to learn to walk on a loose leash and not get to the end of the leash, "If you want your dog to learn to walk on a loose leash, with the leash loose all the time, it must have experience and performance to not get to the end of the leash,'" "Dawn praises and encourages the dog in order to do this when it is also in the field by her side, until the leash can be tightened.."

"Reward the dog with verbal encouragement after three steps and handle it when it is in the place it is practicing, and the leash is free,' Dawn says.

"Then unlock the dog and before driving, start over every time, Say, 'Let's go and give the dog a reward for getting into position."

A Final Word

Choose one of the methods we discussed that works best for you. Try it out for two to three weeks. You should start seeing improvement right away and relatively steady progress, but you may hit a plateau where your dog stops improving for several days. If this happens, give one of the other methods a try. Some dogs respond better when several different positive techniques are used. A puppy with polite leash skills is a joy to walk. Instead of dreading walks, you will look forward to them. Your arm will not hurt, your pup will not gasp, and when people see you walking together, they will admire your puppy's good manners.

Chapter eleven: How to teach some tricks to your dog

The ability to analyze information while giving you more knowledge of how your dog's brain works. Also, teaching him how to do training your dog to learn new tricks stimulates his mind, increases its

tricks is a fun way to spend quality time with your dog, creating a closer bond between you and your buddy.

Do you know that your dog can learn hundreds of words if you apply patience and constant training? For instance, in the following trick called "find the object," your dog will be able to learn how to recognize its toy or a particular item just by recognizing its name. It is a super entertaining game that will widen the vocabulary and activate his thinking process.

Teaching Your Dog To "Find The Object"

What to do:

1) Line up some objects on the floor or a low table and ask your dog to find a specific one.

2) Start with an item that he already knows, such as his food dish or his favorite toy, whatever that may be.

3) Put the object in a conspicuous area right next to two unknown objects, like a newspaper or a piece of wood.

Secondly, point to all the items on the floor or the table and command your dog to "find the dish." By petting his head and perhaps encouraging him as soon as he picks up the right thing, compliment him.. You should use the order to make him hold the dish and lay it down next to you if he knows how to fetch it.

Please do not put the treat on the dish that he brought you because that will encourage him to pick the dish from the objects you laid out. The next thing to do is placing another object on the pile that sounds familiar to your dog (such as a ball). Ask him to find that item and then go back and forth between that second item (a ball) or the dish.

If he chooses the wrong thing, do not scold him, and do not accept it either. Just keep repeating the "find the object." command. Do a more advanced version of the game until he has learned the game, where items are put in various positions, and then instruct him to find it.

Dog Tricks: Paws Crossing

A funny and straightforward trick that you can easily teach your dog or puppy is to cross their paws. Many pets will do this accidentally, and it always puts a smile on our faces when we witness this cute sitting posture.

If you would like to teach your dog how to lie down elegantly with its paws crossed, follow these simple steps:

Step 1: Begin the training with your dog laying down (of course, he should already be trained to do so before attempting the 'cross paws' trick)

Step 2:

1. Ask your dog to give its paw.
2. If he is not trained to respond to this command yet, reach out and grab one of his paws.
3. Click once (using a clicker) and give him a small treat each time. Your dog must remain down while doing this.

Remember: If he still struggles to understand how to give you his paw, use the treat and put it several inches away from one of his paws in the palm of your hand.. He will soon move to touch the treat in your hand, hoping that you will give him the delicious snack. Remember to click every time he reaches your hand.

Step 3: Keep giving his paw to your puppy; make sure you focus only on one paw at a time and do so repeatedly with a click and a reward.

Step 4: Slowly shift your hand closer to your dog's other front paw until your dog has entered a point where you can count on him to hit your hand with one of his paws. He has to lift it now to give you his paw, then step over sideways to meet your hand. What might happen is that he may choose to lift the opposite paw instead of continuing with the trained paw. If this happens, what have to do is pull away from your hand and ignore this response from your dog.

Step 5: You are almost done. Snap your hand back instantly at the last second as your dog will target your hand when it has shifted to the other side near his other leg. His changed paw can now land in a crossed-paw fashion right over the other paw. Make sure that you press and give a treat to.

Step 6: Continue repeating this training regimen, and each time his paw crosses over, slowly fade your hand away, so it is further from the dog. Eventually, your dog will automatically cross his paws when he sees your hand signal and at increasingly longer distances away from you.

Chapter twelve: Getting your dog's attention

The best method to apply is a primary method originated by Mr. William Koehler, a respected animal trainer. His first week's long-line method should be highly considered as one of the best innovations in training dogs.Follow them diligently and accurately, no matter how simple and uncompromising these first-week measures can sound, and you will have a more obedient puppy, one who can understand more easily and quicker.

Send your dog to the backyard, the pavement, or the park on your first training day (only if it offers little or no distraction).

Place the training collar on your dog to make sure it is appropriately fitted. Tie one end of the free ring with the long-line.

Select a position at a distance of around thirty to forty-five feet by gripping the other end of the long-line in your hands.

That may be a can of tin, a fire hydrant, or a specific grass patch.

Walk quickly in a straight line to that spot.

You decide what must stand in your way.

If yours is the kind of canine who is used to having no form of total control placed over him, you can get there will be tricks. He may start wailing, which means that he would fancy going in some other direction, and you are not cooperating with him.

Your dog might roll over on his back and place all four feet in the air, trying to hook a claw in the sky, which means he doesn't particularly want to walk with you because you are not going in the direction he is expecting. He may even try to stop directly in front of you, which means that you forgot to ask his permission to walk, and he'd prefer that you stand still until he's made up his mind.

In dog training, you need to keep one thing clear in mind so that it will also be clear in your dog's mind: you are the master; you are training your dog, not the other way around. Regardless of his tactics, head to the goal you have selected with the end of the long line held tightly in your palm.

That first minute of training (the time it takes you to walk thirty to forty-five feet) may indeed be a test of wills. Your dog wants to make sure you can win this test of wills.
If he learns you will go from point A to point B without acknowledging his opposition, he will establish this assurance. The learning mechanisms will have already been stimulated inside your dog's head by the time you hit your predetermined location, so stand there for about forty-five seconds to a minute. Except for your cat, look about and observe everything about you.

Do not even gaze at him.

Using so will only get you hopelessly embroiled in an emotional fight.

When the forty-five seconds to one minute is over, choose another spot at about the same distance and stroll straight to it at a fast speed without warning or tugging on the leash to get the dog's attention. Again, do not let the dog get in the way of you. If you must clear your throat or attempt to get your dog's attention in some other way before you pass, then your dog is doing a better job of teaching you.

Do not wait for permission from your dog to walk, and go!

Stop again for around forty-five seconds to study your surroundings before you enter your place, but not your puppy.

Again, pick a spot and stroll to it at a brisk pace without any warning.

For the complete fifteen-minute training session, continue with this procedure.Please continue with the same training, and after twenty minutes, get on one knee and untie his collar with the long-line, but do not cut the collar yet. To tell your dog what a wonderful job he is doing just take a few minutes. Give him a nice pat on his back please, and speak with him in an enthusiastic tone of voice. Love him and a scratch on the head of the dog are what you need right now to better shape his temperament for the next lessons that come..

Break

Once you have finished your few minutes of gratitude, remove the training collar casually, and give your dog a little space to take a break and think things over.

While he is unattended, please do not leave the training collar on your dog because the ring will snag items and trigger strangulation. You could have looked unremarkable in the first fifteen minutes of preparation.

If you followed the orders right, though, your dog started to know that he had to travel with you while he was bound to you.

If he has not learned that on his first day, you should be confident that he can learn more by the fourth day because it takes an ordinary dog four days to learn average stuff.

At the same time, there is something else your dog will discover that is equally important.

He is going to learn that you are able to use good judgment and display a will that's much better than his.

Trust and admiration will continue to rise in your actions.

Day 2

Your second day of training should be the same as the first day, except for your pattern direction. The trend could be the opposite of the day before from your starting point because your dog won't know in advance which direction you intend to go. According to your particular dog, you may or may not have struggled on your second day. If you do, behave as you did during the first day. Ignore all distractions and keep walking.

Day 3

Even the most persistent and uncooperative dog will begin to understand by the third day of training that nothing he does will stop you from going in the way you want to go and where you want to go. He's probably going to know that trailing you is the line of least resistance. You might probably note that the dog will be watching you only a little more carefully while you repeat the first two days' practices. He is discovering that while on a leash, he must travel alongside his master. He has discovered that you would not direct your intentions to him. And because he needs to travel with you, he can only be conscious

of your movements in one way, and that is to pay attention to you.

During the fourth day, since you repeat the first three days' procedures, you will discover that there's no more opposition and no games. If your dog tends to get briefly confused and forgetful, this is easy enough.

And that is just what you want to do so that he learns to conquer momentary temptation and diversion and keeps his attention on you. After all, obedience is needed, particularly in a time of emergency. As you will build obedience and a character into your dog, it is not too much to ask that, when other dogs would yield to distraction and temptation, your dog will have his attention place on his master. Using diversion and temptation during your fifteen-minute training sessions is your task from day four before your pet learns to ignore temptation. The methods to follow are the same as the first three days, except that you will walk in the direction of diversion or temptation and hope your dog will rush into it recklessly.

Of course, the exact moment will be selected for you to wish him farewell on his journey, turn and walk quickly in the opposite direction. And, as you might imagine, before he turns around and marches towards you, his path will be quick (fifteen to twenty feet).

Your dog is not going to hate you for having to turn back, so he is not going to equate you with his sudden change of direction at all.

The last four days have showed him that without first testing to see if it is all right with him, you can travel anytime you want and in whichever direction you want. Your dog was sure of this. His mistake existed when for a moment, he took his mind and eyes off you and gave in to temptation. It was also "coincidental" that at the exact moment, and in the opposite direction of what he was going, you wanted to pass. You know that the move was not a coincidence, but that is not what your dog knows, and he will never know. He will know it that is the very moment when a diversion or temptation arises that you will want to change your travel path. Your dog will come to consider any temptation or diversion as a reminder and a prompt to keep his eyes and ears on you if you do your job well for the next few days. People and objects, such as a skateboarder, a strange cat, another dog, a rolling ball, or a plate of food, are obstacles and temptations.

Due to the nature of the dog, the list can be really Kong. It must be considered cruel, however to make someone call your dog by name in an effort to distract him. If you stuck to other circumstances and stuff, it will be best.

Chapter Thirteen: Skills To Teach To Your Dog

Five simple commands that you should teach your dog According to the American Kennel Community, dog discipline is based around the core principles of punishment and incentive.

What is the correction?

This means showing the puppy the distinction between positive and bad behavior. Correcting your dog does not require discipline, physical abuse, or spanking. Saying a definite "No" to your puppy is going to be enough.

What is the reward?

These are therapies offered to the puppy for a job well performed. Such things may be something your dog likes, like a treat or a favorite meal. If your dog is acting, say, "Good dog," then shower it with praise. Before you start teaching, here are five simple commands that your dog will master.

1. The Command "Sit."

The sitting order is the most straightforward and most essential for dog training. It is the foundation for other training techniques.

Instructions

→ Hold a reward treatment in your hand and kneel in front of your dog.

→ Put the food on your pet's nose.

→ Raise your hand upwards.

→ Tell your canine to sit down.

→ If your dog lifts his head to bite the food, use your other hand to guide his back to a sitting position.

→ As it lies down, say, "Sit down."

→ If your pet is meeting the command, applaud it.

→ Repeat this command several times a day.

2. Control of "Heel."

It's a second imperative to teach the dog to heel. This will teach your pet to walk next to you instead of in front of you. His head is with your leg, too. This instruction will show the dog how to stay on a leash properly.

Instructions

→ Your dog's collar and leash.

→ Put the dog in a sitting spot.

→ Hold your leash on your left hand.

→ Put the squeaky toy on the right side of the animal's head.

→ Continue walking in front of the robot when you say the "Heel" order.

→ Catch the attention of your pet by squeaking the animal.

→ If it gets confused or steps in front of you, stop walking immediately.

→ When he pays attention again, he praises your pet and gives them a toy.

→ After your dog has earned you 30 seconds of consideration, start walking again.

→ Increase the time before rewarding your pet.

→ Repeat this cycle every day.

3. Order "down."

This instruction is difficult for dogs to understand. The rewards, though, are fantastic. It can help anxious or frightened dogs to relax.

Instructions

→ Get a nice smelling treat and hold it in your hand.

→ Place your hand on the muzzle of your dog.

→ Allow the treatment to sniff.

→ Move your hand to the floor as your pet smells.

→ Allow your pet to follow suit.

→ If the dog is in a vulnerable state, say "Up."

→ Giving food and attention to your puppy.

→ Perform this instruction every day.

Note: Do not ever move your dog down. When your pet is trying to stand up, say "No," and take your hand down. Finally, the dog is going to find out the right move.

4. The Command "Stay."

This exercise is going to teach your dog self-control.

Instructions

→ Command your pet to sit down.

→ Open your palm and place it in front of you.

→ Say, "Stay here."

→ Step backward.

→ If the dog holds on, show him the treat and the affirmation.

→ Increase the number of steps that you take each time.

→ Please thank your dog for being with you, even if only for a brief period.

5. Command "Leave it."

This command will help a dog stay safe when it's curious about a dangerous object.

Instructions

→ Put the treatment in both hands.

→ Show your puppy that he has a closed fist with a treat inside.

→ Your dog is probably going to try to get the treatment.

→ Say to the companion, "Take it."

→ Give your pet a treat from the other hand once it stops.

→ Wait for your dog to step away from your first-hand next time.

→ Say, "Take it behind."

→ Just offer a treat to the dog as it walks forward. Be sure the eye is in touch with you.

Phase two

Once your dog has mastered the first phase, you will be ready for intermediate training.

→ Using two different treatments of interest in your palm. One is a low-value treatment; the other is a high-value treatment.

→ Place one low-value on the floor.

→ One hand to cover it.

→ Tell your pet, "Leave it."

→ If the dog refuses the medication and paws at you, take the correct medication from the surface.

→ Give him a favorite treat.

→ Thank him for his obedience.

→ After your pet has mastered phase two; you are ready for advanced training. Train the order with a puppy standing up.

→ Use the same measure as before.

Before beginning every training plan, your pet should be well.

Chapter Fourteen: A Healthy Diet For Your Pet

While this section's ethos is about bringing your puppy home and learning the best ways to train him, we must also consider some nutrition and general care fundamentals. A healthy dog is far more able to absorb training information, so your food choice is essential. There are so many food options, and finding the perfect diet is not always easy.

There are so many different types, including:

→ Dry
→ Frozen raw
→ Dehydrated
→ Semi-moist
→ Grain-free etc.

But how do you know you are actually making the right choice for your dog? A little research will go a long way, but you may find that it is trial and error even with the best intentions. Even the most popular and tried and tested brands may not suit your dog. It is worth considering the following:

→ Is your dog reluctant to eat the food you provide?

→ Does your dog have gas?

→ Does the dog's breath smell?

→ Are the dog's teeth dirty?

→ Is the dog's coat dull?

→ Is your dog hyperactive or the opposite, has little energy?

→ Is your dog prone to ear infections or skin infections?

If your dog demonstrates several of the above either frequently or continuously, it is essential to determine why. Each cell of your dog's body requires 45-nutrients to function correctly.
The cells must have:

→ Water

→ Vitamins

→ Minerals

→ Proteins

→ Carbohydrates

→ Fat

These nutrients must have the correct proportions because they aid digestion and, significantly, absorption. This means the cells can receive these vital nutrients more readily. Your dog needs a balanced diet daily. When we talk of nutrients, we must understand that it means to fuel and giving your dog energy. This translates as heat. Nutrients are vital for controlling body temperature. Every aspect of health is determined by the food that you provide and must have the relevant number of calories to grow correctly, to be able to maintain health - all the way into adult life. The nutrients must be sufficient, so your dog can reproduce or grow to a right old age.

Puppies grow incredibly fast. Their weight from birth can multiply 15-40 times. Of course, this can be different according to the breed of dog. Skeletal development is almost complete by the time your puppy reaches one year of age. With all this growth and development, it is vital to have the right food. Puppies tend to eat a lot more food than an adult dog. This is especially important so to cope with the growth spurts that occur. Nutritional deficiencies that occur at a young age can create health issues when older.

The growing stage of larger dog breeds can continue growing until four years of age approximately. Your puppy's development is at its most critical during the two-seven months of age. There are many physical stresses during this time, so your puppy must have the right food to ensure a healthy functioning immune system. You must also buy the food that has been manufactured for your puppy's stage of development. This means that you should not give senior dog food to puppies.

Puppy food contains more protein than the foods specifically for adult dogs. Manufacturers are aware of how much protein is needed during this tender age, and food should be carefully balanced with calcium, phosphorus, and magnesium.

Look at the label on the food and note the animal proteins. Check the listings for the first five ingredients. Unfortunately, many available dog foods have inadequate magnesium, calcium, and phosphorus ratios. When selecting food for your puppy, you must consider the protein percentage as dogs do need meat to be healthy. Dog's teeth are meant for tearing and chewing meat. The digestive process (unlike ours) starts in the stomach with enzymes made to break down raw food and meat.

Protein

Protein is essential and in dog food, consider where the protein comes from. A combination is often found in grains or plants, but you will also have an additional protein, often chicken or beef. Different types of meat will have different protein levels. Chicken and fish have the highest protein levels, but foods that are too high in protein may not be as good as you think and, just as flawed as providing food that is too low in proteins. It is a real balancing act. If you feed your puppy food that is too high in proteins, it can damage their kidneys. So, for most dogs, beef-based foods can be used as a maintenance diet and are useful for any dog that needs surgery or healing. Chicken-based foods are acceptable. If your dog does not like beef, then you can opt for lamb-based foods. Fish-based foods should be avoided for regular use as they are too high in proteins and will mean that the puppy's kidneys have to work too hard.

Consider the activity level of your dog. If you have a working breed - a toy or terrier, they will need higher animal protein levels.

Amino acids

Amino acids can be defined as building blocks of protein. When heated, they are all but destroyed. Unfortunately, all dry and canned foods are heated, and so, the proteins within these foods are chemically changed. As a result, amino acids will be deficient. It is better to have frozen or freeze-dried foods as these are more natural.

The symptoms of deficiency are similar to the symptoms of excessive proteins and include:

→ Reproductive stress - heart, kidneys, liver, thyroid, adrenal glands,and the bladder.
→ A dull coat
→ Too much shedding
→ Vomiting or diarrhea
→ Slow healing following surgery or from injury
→ Kidney problems
→ Poor appetite.
→ Tail chasing or spinning
→ Poor pigmentation
→ Chronic skin or ear infections
→ Aggressive behavior

Carbohydrates

Carbohydrates are found in grains and root vegetables and are essential for dogs for correct digestion. The carbohydrates are broken down into starch. Then, into simple sugars and glucose. These are needed for energy but are also vital for your puppy's brain development. Carbohydrates are essential for stool formation and the thyroid too. High dosages are not necessary. A low carbohydrate diet, one that is high in protein, is much better. Consider oats, wheat, or barley. Brown rice is also good. Corn is commonly used, but it is used in many lower quality foods.

Avoid lots of dog foods with soy as a carbohydrate because it is high in protein, making nutrients challenging to absorb.

Try to aim for consistency with the diet. Although you may wish to change your dog's food if it does not take to the food you are generally giving, it is wise to change food over slowly. A quick change of diet can harm digestion. If you wish to try your dog on raw vegetables at some point, do so a little at a time. If you have been feeding on a different diet for a while, it may be that the dog's stomach acid and digestive juices are not as strong as they need to be. This means food will not digest as well. It is wise to cook the vegetables at first lightly. Do this for about a week, then reduce the cooking time gradually. Eventually, your dog will be on raw foods.

Both saturated and polyunsaturated fats are essential for your dog. Saturated fats in Omega 3 is obtained through animal sources. Polyunsaturated fats – Omega 6 comes from vegetable sources. Saturated fat is good for energy, so if you have a dog who requires many exercises, they will need to eat approximately 20% animal fat. If your dog has insufficient levels of fat in the diet, you may see the following:

→ Low energy levels

→ Dry skin

→ Cell damage

→ Heart problems

→ Growth problems

→ Too much animal fat in the diet leads to:

→ Obesity

→ Cancer

Polyunsaturated fats can be found in vegetable sources. Look for sunflower oil, olive oil, corn oil, flaxseed oil, and so on. These are essential for a healthy coat and skin. Note: if your dog is itching or scratching or detecting skin lesions on the belly or the legs, there may be a lack of polyunsaturated fats in the diet.

Linoleic acid is one of three essential fatty acids. Give your dog safflower or flaxseed oil as these are the least allergenic. Check how to store flaxseed oil as, if not careful, it can become rancid. These oils are much preferred to corn oil.

Vitamins

There are fat-soluble vitamins, including A, E, and K. These are stored in the fatty tissues of the body. They are also stored in the liver. Water-soluble vitamins include B and C. These help to break down the proteins. These are then filtered and expelled via the kidneys. This usually takes between 4 and 8 hours once the food has been consumed.

Minerals are also needed, but they are still the most critical nutrients, although only small amounts are essential. Minerals help with body fluids; they form blood and bones; they help with the nervous system. They also function as coenzymes along with vitamins. When you open food, try to keep it in an airtight place. This is important because when you open a bag of food and are exposed to the elements, any vitamins and minerals start to break down. Store in a dark place too. Vitamins B and C are depleted the most.

Water

Your puppy must have plenty of freshwaters. This is so important as it cannot survive more than a few days without it. A dog could survive weeks without food, although this would be unhealthy and dangerous. Water is used for the digestive process and helps to break down food. It aids the absorption of nutrients. Water helps the regulation of body temperature and keeps the blood acid levels constant while also removing any toxic substances.

While training your puppy, you may need to limit water access after 8 pm so that the puppy does not have to go outside regularly. Both you and the puppy need to sleep. Use a heavy grade steel bowl or a glass bowl as this keeps the water fresh. Try to avoid using ceramic bowls as they may leach lead into the water.

Digestion

When you choose pet food, it is essential to disregard advertising instead of focusing on the label's ingredients. It is not about cost. You may choose a branded food that costs more, but it may not be as good. A raw food diet may cost more, but the ingredients will be better. Your dog will be much healthier. Raw, frozen, or dehydrated foods pass through into the intestinal tract within 4 1/2 hours. This means that your dog benefits from the energy gained from these foods quickly. These are perhaps the best diets because they are more easily digested.

If you buy tinned foods like those in the supermarket, it will take about 9 hours to pass through the stomach. For most pets, this slower digestion is not so important. The digestive system of a dog is much shorter than our own. This means food consumed is processed much more readily. A dog's stomach acid is strong and kills any bacteria that enters it. If your dog is unwell or is switching over to a raw diet, it is essential to transition the food. This helps to rebuild stomach acid and to deal with higher levels of bacteria. Buy meat suitable for human consumption from a good supermarket.

Are you worried about how much to feed your puppy?

Ideally, give three small meals a day at first. You will gradually notice that the amount of food consumed tends to settle. If needed, miss out on the lunchtime meal but be guided by your puppy. Remember, this is a crucial developmental stage—feed morning and night.

Four kinds of food that can be dangerous for your dog

Many items are poisonous to a dog and also potentially fatal if eaten, despite possessing immensely powerful stomachs that can normally tackle anything pulled out of a garbage can. Many of them are not only human food, but things you wouldn't normally want a dog to consume in your home. What follows is a list of things that you can do to keep your dog safe or away from.

Human Food

Although dogs can take on and digest a lot of human foods well there are others that they do not consume. These include chocolate, onions, individual grains, garlic, beer, and others, among other foods, are wary about feeding pork. Some foods contain chemicals (such as theobromine in chocolate) and acidic properties such as onions that can cause liver and pancreatic complications with gas and indigestion issues. While a minimum sum is not actually going to kill your dog, it is not going to kill him, it doesn't do him any good, so it is best to secure these items and others from him.

Medications

Of course, for dogs, any substance can be risky. Like with kids who do not know any better, whether they are left out or tossed into the garbage, a dog may get into medications. When it breaks, some dogs might only be chewing on the bottle, so they unintentionally swallow it. Still hold medicines tightly stored in a high cabinet that is out of sight, as well as antacids and children's medication.

Plants

There are also numerous domestic trees and shrubs poisonous to dogs. In an effort to calm their stomachs, canines will occasionally munch on the greenery while they make grass outside. But some of these plants have toxins in dogs that may induce illness. Ferns, daffodil bulbs, lilies, and dracaena are among the most common species. There are also individual garden plants, such as Ivy/vines, Yew, Foxgloves, Onion, and Tomato plants, among many others, that may be growing outdoors to damage them. Thinking on what could possibly hurt your dog is a good thing.

Household cleaners

Normally, you wouldn't expect your dog to get into your household cleaners, but your dog could confuse them for toys and start playing and chewing with the brightly colored plastic bottle and the fact that they are stored in a low cupboard under the sink. It is dangerous to anything containing chemicals, particularly bleach, and lethal to anything like drain cleaner or oven cleaner. If you think your dog has played with something (tellale sign will be teeth marks on the bottle), for guidance and assistance, you must contact a vet and animal poison control. When it comes to domestic cleaners, it could make the difference in his life.

Like children, dogs can get into trouble quickly, and they will usually find anything that you didn't want them too! Therefore, you must always dog-proof your house before getting a dog and practice common sense from there on by keeping things safe and secure and out of paws-reach! However, even then, they can still get into mischief and swallow something they shouldn't, so always be aware.

Chapter fifteen: General Do's and Don'ts's

Canine preparing can be challenging for the unenlightened - both proprietor and pet - however, it's, at last, a remunerating experience for Individuals who endure. These canine preparing rules and regulations will help you maintain a strategic distance from common traps when preparing your puppy.

Do discover an interruption-free area.

Continuously start learning another order at an area that is liberated from interruptions. This will enable your puppy to concentrate on learning. After she comprehends the direction, present interruptions gradually.

Remember to prize for good conduct.

Many pooch proprietors reward their canines while adapting. However, they rapidly neglect to remunerate their canine for proceeding with excellent conduct. "Directions like 'remain' and 'drop it' are conceivably lifesaving," says hound coach Lindsay Justin. "It is imperative to fortify the significance of following these directions each time you use them by remunerating fittingly."

Do utilize both hand and verbal prompts.

Visual impairment and loss of hearing are chronic pains for more established mutts. By utilizing the two prompts, you can hold the capacity to speak with your pet.

Try not to anticipate sessions longer than 20 minutes. Anticipating that a youthful canine should concentrate on learning for longer than 20 minutes is unjustifiable. Instead, attempt to set aside 20 minutes to work with your canine every day. As your canine arrives at development, her capacity to focus will develop, enabling you to expand sessions on the off chance that you wish.

Do rehearse directions in various areas.

"Youthful canines do not have a clue about that 'sit' and 'remain' in general, regardless of where you are," Justin says. "For them, 'remain' rehearsed inside the house may have little association with a 'remain' in the patio." Try rehearsing at different places, so your canine will connect the order with your voice and hand signals and not the area.

Try not to utilize an energized voice to pick up your pet's consideration. An energized voice may assist you with getting your puppy to come to you from the outset. However, it would be best if you did not go after your canine's consideration. Utilize a firm, quiet voice to give directions and do not rehash the signal. This will guarantee that the pup will come to you in any event, when something different she sees is all the more energizing. Do strengthen pack conduct consistently.

Your puppy ought to see you as the leader of your home before you start preparing. The building that relationship necessitates that you strengthen excellent conduct and rebuff awful conduct reliably. Ensuring your puppy is behaving during everyday strolls is likewise a decent method to fabricate that bond.

Try not to be reluctant to go to a pooch coach.
Regardless of whether you do not take a crack at a standard multi-week compliance course, think about booking a couple of meetings with a pooch mentor. A coach will have the option to understand your canine's mind that will make preparing simpler.

To remain quiet, regardless.
Pooch preparing requires a great deal of tolerance and uplifting feedback. Never holler at or hit your canine; you need to move steadfastness, not fear.

Try not to stop until progress has been made.
"Numerous proprietors become baffled and quit preparing before the canine has taken in the direction," Justin says. This can fortify awful conduct in a pup, making her imagine that misbehaving can get her out of preparing.

Chapter Sixteen: How To Teach Your Dog To Shake Hands

First of all, when you go to start any training series with your pet, you are relaxed and do not hurry! It is essential since the animal will notice any hint of stress or anxiety that you generate on your part, and the dog will be more aware of your mood than what you want to teach him. If you feel angry or frustrated, you better leave the exercises with your dog for another day and that dogs often perceive these moods right away. And more if they are negative.

1. The first thing you have to do is stand in front of the animal and make it feel. Better if you also feel at their level. If you do not know how to make your dog feel through voice command, you better wait for your pet to feel at home, take advantage of the moment, and stand in front of him.
2. Then take a piece of sausage or a "chuche" and show it to your furry friend. When you realize that you have the treat, you close your hand not to be eaten. Always do this in front of him and with your arm extended in front of your head.

3. Move your hand with the prize inside the clenched fist so that the animal is interested in it and wants to eat the candy you have hidden. At the same time, you say a voice command, the one you want, always the same, as "chócala" to associate the command with the action of giving the leg.

Why?

Dogs usually act to this challenge to access the inside of your fist with your mouth several times and not succeed. Next, he will try to take the "church" that you have stored with his legs. Do you follow me?

4. When your dog's paw touches your hand (believe me, he will try), you immediately say "good" (you can also use a clicker, it is easier for him), and then you open your hand and let him eat his prize, that He has done very well.

5. Afterwards, it is only a matter of practicing these steps three or four times for two or three days, and that's it! A few times that you continue with the training, you will see that your dog offers you the leg when listening to the word you have chosen, even before seeing your hand with the prize inside.

What if my dog gets stuck or ignores me?

Not all dogs are the same; it happens to us that there are more creative and less.

... Well, if your pet does not catch it at first (a low and difficult thing to happen), follow these tips:

If you have tired of practicing these training pieces and your dog still ignores you, you will have to facilitate the matter. Shake your hand with the candy inside (step 3), but this time you bring the closed fist in motion to its leg, a span or less. You will see how this time if he listens to you and gets this way, your pet learns to shake hands with the voice of the command you want.

If, after all this, your furry partner still does not "catch it," you can try the following:

Repeat steps 1, 2, and 3. And then take his leg with your other hand, put it at the height of your clenched fist and shout "well" (or use the clicker) and then reward him with another puppy. Repeat this last step several times and when you master it, return to the initial training from the beginning (step 1). You will see how he understands you now and does it well.

Very important...

Like almost all workouts, it is to have patience and repeat several times all that is necessary. And above all, remember that they have to be short sessions, and repeat them three or four times a day. If you do not follow these parameters and exceed the sessions or their time, your dog will get bored or frustrated. With what you will eventually get nothing. Moreover, if you see that after repeating two or three times, the animal loses interest or becomes overwhelmed, for training until the next day, the key is a few short sessions every day. It is a matter of regularity more than anything else. Do not forget to end the sessions by filling your pet with pampering and affection, no matter how well he has done. It's about associating workouts as a positive. It is no use pissing off, getting sober, and repeating to satiety throughout the afternoon. Many less screaming or hitting. Then you will never learn.

And when I stop giving prizes by hand?
This is important. You will have to stop teaching your fist with the hidden prize at any given time so that it gives you the leg. How? It's simple...

No more "sweets."
A- Show your pet your fist with a hidden prize. (Repeat steps 1, 2, and 3) As soon as you kick, you offer the prize but with the other hand, NOT WITH THE CLOSED FIST. And repeat this several times.
B- Then you repeat the first three steps, but this time when you show him the fist with the prize inside, and you say, "fuck it, let it be an open hand and without a bump, and when you give it a leg you give it a prize with the other hand, as in step A. And now it's just a matter of repeating this several times until you learn it.
C- Well, when you see that your pet has learned well that by saying "chócala," he paws and rewards you, you stop giving him prizes little by little

For example, start repeating the exercise three times and only reward him The first time and the last. In a couple of days, you only reward him the third time, and in another couple of days, you stop doing it, and instead of a food prize, you caress him and give him pampering. You will see how soon he forgets the "sweets" and conforms as a prize with your touch.

And ready. In addition to having a good time and joining more in tune with your pet, it will shake your hand just by saying "chócala" And not only that, your friends and other people who know your dog can also do it. And it is that these training exercises usually work with other people around the animal, once you have taught them.

Chapter Seventeen: Planning A Trip With Your Dog

Taking your dog on a journey requires a bit of thinking; you need to be sure if your dog is ready both physically and mentally. Ask your self in certainty if the dog can tolerate it, but making it fly for many hours to stay in their little house once they arrive is not fair to either.

Before Travelling

Make sure you inquire about how welcome your dog will be in your destination. Cultures are different; do not forget that. Visit your veterinarian, make sure your vaccinations are up to date and get updated copies of the health records for your trip. Your veterinarian must confirm that the dog is in good health for traveling.

Ensure you know if there are any health issues (that is, insects, cold, heat) at the destination and take the necessary precautions.

Packing For The Trip

Take your dog's health and vaccination certificates against rabies (they are needed when crossing few borders).

The photo you should use will be recent of the dog for identification if it is lost.

Put your plate of food, the drinking fountain, the belt, the toys, the little house, the medicines, and the cleaning equipment in the suitcase.

You must bring your food if you travel by car or if you are not sure of getting it at the destination. Sudden dietary changes can cause digestive disorders and ruin the trip for your pet and yourself.

Ensure that your dog has its identification plagues, with your contact written on it and preferably that of the place of destination.

Travel By Land

→ It's easier to have a doghouse or a dog carrier in your vehicle's rear. Do not expose it to sunlight directly.

→ If the dog is out of the carrier, make sure the buckled belt is in place. Unique harnesses are attached to the seat belt for sale. If the gear stops suddenly, serious injury could occur, do not use a leash.

→ Do not leave your dog in the van's open box.

→ Do not feed your pet for at least 3 hours before you start your journey.

→ Give your fresh dog water to drink during the stops. For being such a good travel companion, you can also reward him with a treat.

→ Feed your dog shortly after arriving or stopping for the remainder of the day.

→ Wear a leash before you leave the vehicle.

→ NEVER leave your pet alone in a closed vehicle. Heat and insufficient air circulation can quickly cause heat stress or even death.

Air Travel

→ When delays and transfers are more extended, try to avoid times of increased activity to travel.

→ Organize a trip with as few stops and transfers as possible.

→ Make your dog's hotel and air bookings well in advance.

→ Some airlines permit small dogs to travel with their owners (usually at an additional cost) if the carrier fits under their seat.

Otherwise, rent or purchase a carrier or small house that complies with the airline's regulations and attach an adhesive label with the LIVE ANIMAL legend. Write your name and address and the gender of the person that your dog can contact at the intended location if necessary. Place a blanket or pillow at the base of the structure. Add water to the house door with a drinker. The tank is meant to be deep and not too full of water to avoid spillage.

Take your dog for a tiring walk during the flight day before you leave for the airport.

→ At the end of the trip, immediately pick up your pet.

→ The dog can spend some time in quarantine in some foreign locations. Find out the country you plan to travel to with your travel agent or consulate on this page.

At The Destination

→ It complies with all pet regulations at the holiday spot. When you leave your dog alone, leave your dog in a small house, carrier, or limited space. Collect your waste quickly. Your consideration is going to help pets stay as guests..

Chapter eighteen: Periodic Health check

Periodic checks

Veterinarians often only see pets for puppy or kitten tests and legally prescribed immunizations. Many pet owners understand that modern veterinary medicine has developed resources that enable veterinarians to identify and manage various diseases traditionally thought to be merely failing health due to old age, with euthanasia being the only human remedy. With routine veterinarian checks and early care, yesterday's old age and the end of life for a pet are now the new middle age breed, with more years of good health and fitness left for the breed to enjoy with their family.

The Seven Hills Veterinary Hospital urges pet owners looking forward to years of safe and enjoyable companionship with their dog or cat to pay careful thought to animal care checks on their pet twice a year. Every year, the first visit is a health check-up and a discussion of any changes in the pet's behavior or daily routine. The second appointment, which takes place six months away, consists of a wellness test and a study of the pet's dietary needs.

If your pet is due for any vaccinations, they will be administered during these twice-yearly tests. We adopt a three-year vaccine regimen at the Seven Hills Veterinarian Hospital because we do not believe in over-vaccination. Before prescribing any vaccines, we ask you to complete the disease risk evaluation questionnaire and ensure that we establish an exact vaccine schedule personalized to the needs of your pet and your lifestyle.

The health programs also include a range of early warning treatments, including blood testing to determine nutritional disorders before your pet shows acute symptoms, enabling you to take early action; fecal checks to locate internal infections that may eventually spread to humans; and heartworm checks. We are confident you willl consider twice-yearly veterinarian wellness tests for your pet to be a safe investment in money invested in the long term and, most specifically, in a happier and safer life that your pet will share with you.

Vaccines
Why does my pet need vaccinations?

Puppies and kittens are bred with weak immune systems that make them particularly vulnerable to disease. Fortunately, their mothers transfer part of their immunity to them through the colostrum when they nurse. Colostrum is a material present in the milk of the mother for the first few days after birth. It provides essential protective proteins to her newborns against several diseases. These agents are referred to as "maternal antibodies." So long so maternal antibodies against a particular disease are present in the infant's body, they may continue to protect against the disease.

Nevertheless, these antibodies can also make other forms of vaccines inactive against different diseases during the time they are working. How long these maternal antibodies last vary between individuals and are affected by many factors. We assume that maternal antibodies are gone, on average, around 16-20 weeks of age. Therefore, the standard puppy/kitten vaccination sequence starts at about 6-8 weeks of age. Boosters are given every 2-4 weeks until about 16-20 weeks of age in the hope of reducing the window of opportunity for infection. This window of opportunity is when maternal antibodies wear out and vaccination will activate the immune response of the person to a disease. A single dose of either vaccine could be expected if animals are above 20 weeks of age.. The frequency of sickness and mortality is considerably higher in regions where the vaccine is not routinely practiced. It is particularly true of Canine and Feline Distemper, Canine Parvovirus and Rabies.

When much is my cat supposed to be vaccinated?

While it was common practice in Australia to have your pet vaccinated every 12 months, new studies have shown that some vaccinations have been useful for more than a year. The waiting period for each injection will depend on the age of your pet. If the pet is a puppy or a cat, it will usually be shot three times in a six-month cycle, and after that, it may be a regular or even a three-year cycle. In most cases, critical vaccines are given every three years or even later if accompanied by animal conditions and the environment. Because each animal should be treated as a unique being, it is a good idea to take your pet to a vet and have the vaccination protocol prescribed for catering to meet your pet's specific requirements. Sufficient contact and regular appointments with your doctor are all critical to the safety of your animals.

When do I continue the vaccination of my pet?
If you have kittens or dogs, the first round of vaccinations (usually two to three vaccines) is issued at about six to eight weeks of age. Nevertheless, the final vaccine will not be given until the pet is sixteen weeks old. This is because antibodies in the breast milk of the mother can interfere with vaccinations. A title test may also be performed to check if your adult dog or cat needs vaccination. This is an affordable test that will measure the number of antibodies present in your pet's system, revealing a need for a booster of immunity. Your Vet will provide you with more detail about the title checks.

Would that sound like a lot of shots to you? Okay, is it?
Yes! Yes! Vaccinating and preventing diseases such as parvovirus in a puppy is much cheaper than treating it. There is rarely any

assurance that the puppy will survive, even with the best possible care. On average, the puppy/kitten receives 3-4 sets of vaccines in its puppy/kitten sequence, based on the age at which the vaccines first began. This is likely that others can earn more if they start at a very early age.

Would that mean the more regular boosters will be much better? Taking vaccines so early (less than two weeks apart) does not give the body time to respond appropriately to vaccinations. If the vaccine booster is administered too early, the body's immune reaction to the first vaccine will interfere with the second vaccine's reaction; thus, the second vaccine's intended booster effect does not improve the immune response. While vaccinations would preferably be spaced by at least two weeks of intervals, it should be remembered that specific shelters may need to send vaccinations at near intervals due to situations specific to the sheltered climate. Your veterinarian can inform you if they consider any additional boosters after taking a pet.

Would the vaccine ensure that my cat will never develop the disease?

No, no. Many factors affect the immune response of the animal to the vaccines. We recognize that certain vaccines will only mitigate the symptoms of the disease (e.g., Bordetella, Feline Herpes, and Calici viruses). We recognize that a relatively limited percentage of animals will never react to vaccines, no matter how many they get. These animals are known as non-responsible animals. The truth remains, though, that many more species are safe from illness because they are vaccinated.

What vaccinations will my pet be given?

Through vaccination, the pet will receive various factors, such as illness type, age, diet, local laws, and any prior adverse effects or health problems exacerbated by immunizations. Vaccines are generally categorized as Core and Noncore. At the Pet Health Department, we use the American Animal Hospital Association (AAHA) recommendations for dogs and the American Feline Practice Association (AAFP) recommendations for cats.

1. Key vaccines are intended to protect against pathogens that cause severe illness and death and for which the bulk of the population is at risk of contracting. Types include Canine Distemper, Canine Parvovirus, Canine Adenovirus, Panleukopenia (feline distemper), Rhinotracheitis (feline herpes), and Feline Calicivirus. Critical vaccines can also be mandated by legislation (i.e., rabies).

2. Noncore vaccines are those diseases for which the climate of an organism gives him a greater chance of being exposed to. Most, but not all, of these diseases will cause severe illness or even death to your pet. Based on where you live, some of these could be transferred to the "heart" group due to a higher incidence of disease in that region (i.e., Lyme).

3. Bordetella, Lyme, Canine Influenza (H3N8 and H3N2), Parainfluenza, and Crotalus atrox toxoid (rattlesnake vaccine) are non-core canine vaccines. Um, ii.FeLV, Chlamydophila felis, Bordetella bronchiseptica contain feline noncore vaccines

Vaccines not approved are those that are deemed unsafe for several reasons. Types for dogs are coronavirus. Examples for cats are FIP. Specific treatments include cancer vaccines for canine melanoma and lymphoma. There are corrective vaccinations, not prevention ones, used by others for therapy.

How often should my pet receive vaccinations?

This may be different according to the type of vaccination, age, diet, local laws, and other health factors. We also have evidence demonstrating that critical vaccinations can induce immunity that will last for many years if the correct vaccination sequence has been delivered. In general, puppies and kittens receive their primary vaccines from around 6-8 weeks of age and are boosted every 3-4 weeks to around 16-20 weeks of age. They will be boosted again one year later and every three years after that, or they will perform annual titles. Acceptable procedures for adult dogs with no prior history of vaccination are either a sequence of two DA2PP vaccinations or a single dose of a combined live or recombinant DA2PP vaccine. We are then improved one year back and every three years after that (or annual titles). Adult cats are expected to receive a series of 2 FVRCP vaccines.

When the initial dose of rabies has been given, one year after, the patient will get a booster. Age (12 weeks vs. adult) would not modify the booster provision one year after at the time of the first vaccination or form of vaccine (1 year vs. 3 year vaccine). The type of vaccine used (1 year vs. three years) and state or municipal requirements decide future booster cycles.

Noncore vaccine intervals are usually one year. However, certain vaccines (i.e., Bordetella) can be shorter due to an increased risk of infection and the likelihood of immunity not lasting for a full year. It's best to work with your veterinarian and tailor a schedule of vaccines to suit your pet's individual needs.

Primary effects or side effects

Since vaccinations activate the immune system of the patient, mild reactions can often occur afterward. The most frequent symptoms occur within the first few hours of vaccination, including allergic reactions, inflammation to the vaccine region, and fever, which usually appear over a day or two. Less likely side effects include vaccine-related immune disease or small granulomas (tumors) at the injection site. These granulomas should be closely watched.

If you see that your pet has any of the following signs for longer than two days, send them to the Vet immediately:

- Weakness:
- trouble breathing
- Vomiting;
- lack of appetite;
- Diarrhoea
- Uncommon side effects of vaccination may include:
- hemolytic anemia;
- Issues of the reproductive system
- Interim limping (in cats)
- Sarcomas (in cats): Sarcomas can be one of the worst side effects of vaccination; however, these tumors are mainly associated with a form of the vaccine not regularly administered in Australia. Fast diagnosis will lead to successful tumor elimination, so oversee your cat to ensure it stays healthy.

Chapter nineteen: Muscle Building Training

The human body is so complex that needs the care to function at peak standards. In early human history, the daily rigors of life from day to day supported the human body with all the fitness and aerobic activity is required. This forced training helped to build muscle and increase stamina. The closest companions of everyday humans, dogs, often have a complicated mechanism requiring training and upkeep to work at optimal levels.

If your dog is a house pet, does hard labor on family grounds, or participates in dog shows, strength training plays a vital part in your dog's life. Providing fitness and physical instruction to your dog can not only enhance your everyday routine, but it will also guarantee that your dog can work anytime you want/need to do so without any complications.

How Physical Exercise Matters for Dogs

When you go to the gym or take the woods for a stroll, you are bound to do so in an attempt to boost your general wellbeing. The same is right of the horse. Improving their physical wellbeing is the most critical advantage of rigorous exercise. Physical training will help keep the body weight right for your dog. If your dog keeps a healthy body weight, it can cope with less pain in its joints. Regular exercise, such as physical conditioning, will also reduce the amount of fat in the dog's body. Protein is an established cause of inflammation in the joints of your dog. It ensures that proper body weight by physical exercise not only decreases the burden of obesity on your dog's knees; it also eliminates the risk of inflammation from fat deposits.

Last but not least, weight training offers the additional advantage of improved body density and physical strength. As a result, the dog's muscles should help defend and facilitate the mobility of its joints and enhance its quality of life. In conclusion, consider the other benefits of strength training:
Stronger muscle and skeletal structures, as well as tendons and other connective tissues to resist damage. Eat your calories and increase your metabolic rate. This helps the dog to shed weight and protect against potential weight gain.

Increased success in competitive sports and work roles.
What's Strength Training?
As the name implies, your dog's strength training focuses on an exercise routine that specializes in helping your body improve strength, muscle mass, and endurance. Training in strength for dogs is not that different from training in strength for humans.

Sure, you are probably hitting the gym, lifting weights, and sneaking a glimpse of yourself in the mirror.

Your dog will not stand and flex in front of the mirror, but the idea is the same. The aim is to work with your dog to have incremental resistance levels to promote muscle development and increased strength. Bodyweight workouts, not including cycling or running, are the main types of movement in a strength training routine. Running or jumping, without extra weight, is known as aerobic exercise.

Strength Training Options for your Dog

Now that you know the benefits of strength training and what it is, you are no doubt wondering where to start. While humans expend thousands of dollars on gym equipment and membership, you can provide your dog's strength training with little financial investment. There are many strategies open to you when you try to strengthen your dog's muscle mass and power, and the following choices are some traditional strength training exercises that offer a decent starting point.

Hills.

You have all the information required to continue your dog's strength training routine, whether you live in a hilly neighborhood or have any nearby.. Running up a hill with your dog utilizes gravity as a means of resistance, creating muscle strength and enhancing your dog's general fitness.

Weighted Jacket

In recent years, a popular choice, especially among owners of working breeds, is to take dogs for a walk or to run with weighted jackets strapped on their backs. The benefit of a weighted jacket is the potential to turn every exercise into a strength training regimen. Every object can be inserted in the vest to serve as protection, and the vest can be worn when swimming, driving, playing, or jumping around in the backyard. The theory is that weight provides strength to some form of movement.

Squats

Believe it or not, the dog will do squat drills to reinforce the muscles of the body. Today, there are a variety of ways this can be achieved. The best approach is to use medications that the dog jumps to catch or receive. Start by asking your dog to lay down or lie down. Keeping a treat above their mouth, let them hop up for a reward. Between three bounces, praise the actions of your puppy, and repeat. Each jump challenges the leg muscles of your dog to grow and strengthen.

Sprinting

You and the dog both need to be in decent physical shape for sprinting to work. If both parties are in shape, sprinting is a great technique to build muscle tone and strength while improving overall fitness. As a human, you are going to have to be out front to lead the sprinting exercise. Be sure your dog is well trained, or this practice will quickly turn into play and lose concentration on sprinting.

Significant reminder

Your dog's anatomy is like the own anatomy in several ways. Bear in mind that you cannot just go to the gym and start pushing a bench of 300 lbs. Or maybe squatting 200 lbs. Your dog requires to be eased into a strength training period. It is essential to use a progressive scale that increases the difficulty of your dog's regimen over time.

Conclusion

When you have taught your puppy to pay attention, basic obedience training will be as straightforward as watching your puppy doing anything you enjoy and praising your feeding habits. E.g., if your puppy sits happily, praise it, or if it lies down, you may want to praise the action. If you want to teach the puppy to respond to hand gestures or verbal orders, then you can use food as an incentive to get the puppy to the place you like, and then release the food after the puppy has demonstrated the action. It is best not to use verbal orders until the puppy has mastered the action you are teaching. When the action is performed relatively consistently, you can add a verbal order before making a hand gesture.

Again, you don't want your puppy to do anything only because food is there, so it's better to start decreasing food at this stage; too-begin by using a hand gesture with no food in it. If the puppy has done what you told you to do, you will offer the award as a gift on the other side. And now you are bringing your hand signs. Just use the food as a reward for the second sitting, then the third sitting, and so forth, until the puppy has been conditioned to sit down without the food being present. And even food incentives will continue to be overshadowed by play sessions, pats or something else that your puppy enjoys.

Puppy training can be concise sessions with just two to three rehearsals in one activity, and then wind up with a puppy showing excellent behavior. So maybe you will find the puppy lying down, give him a carrot, and that is it. It is just taking advantage of a dog providing a trait that can be repeated to increase the probability of the behavior happening again. If you do so many at once, the puppy is going to lose confidence. Young dogs have the attention span of a dog, so make the most of watching your pet enjoying anything you enjoy and praising that's a perfect way to house your puppy's training rather than long training hours. Keeping it brief means that it's easier to concentrate on some excellent research and keep it enjoyable and comfortable for both you and the puppy.

Another trick is to use the puppy's meal as an incentive for good behavior, and instead of enjoying a feeding dish, expect the puppy to compete with his treats. When you're spoon-feeding your puppy for good behavior, you would also like to encourage your puppy to be polite when getting food out of your spoon rather than snatching and loud chewing. Yeah, you are.

 You are teaching your puppy for two issues here, eating food entirely out of your hand as well as acting out.

And you can see that puppy training does not mean systematic dog obedience training, but it's something that can be initiated as soon as you get your new puppy home. Through first teaching your puppy to rely on you and to respond to his name, Teaching A Puppy To Respond To His Name-Having Fun With Your Puppy, you are setting in motion the first step stone to more obedience. It's also something you don't need to schedule long periods for because catching the puppy in the act of doing anything you enjoy and rewarding it so that the puppy may replicate the conduct.

All dogs deserve good care and do not have to be arduous or costly to train the puppy. If you are sharing your house with a new puppy or an elderly dog, it is never too early to continue your dog training. Most dogs are happy with the stability and trust that comes from teaching.

Dogs want more than anything to make their owners happy that is why they train efficiently. Before you start, make a list of the basic commands you want to teach: "Sitting," "still," "come," "down," or "no" (always useful commands). You can also control the king, teach them not to order food, and avoid the house's accidents. All this can be done-you need consistency, praise, occasional rewards, a lot of patience, and positivism.

Be cautious and forward-looking in the event of an accident while teaching a dog to go to the bathroom. This is one of your dog's most important things to teach, starting with a program. Hogs are typical animals, so take them to the toilet after feeding, playing, waking up from a nap, before going to bed, or looking for a place to urinate and add these moments into the system.

When the dog is in the right place, laud him a lot. Next time only snacks are going to be motivated. The puppy will learn when and when to do that as time goes on. Remember, it is not all perfect puppies.

When you first start focusing on dog training, it can feel daunting. If you are uncertain where to get going, create a week-by-week plan to organize yourself better. Select one or two key commands every week to focus on. Prepare to make any changes to the dog's lifestyle to avoid or change issues with behavior.